MW01618110

# THE ORIGINAL PEOPLE

*THE ANCIENT CULTURE AND WISDOM OF THE LENNI-LENAPE PEOPLE*

**THE ORIGINAL PEOPLE:**

THE ANCIENT CULTURE AND WISDOM

OF THE LENNI-LENAPE PEOPLE

BY CHIEF QUIET THUNDER AND GREG VIZZI

AS TOLD TO MARCIA ADAMS AND GREG VIZZI

**Nature's Wisdom Press**

First Revision, First Print Edition: October, 2020



ISBN 978-17350457-0-2



For more information, please visit:

www.Natures-Wisdom.com

## DEDICATION: FOR THE YOUNG PEOPLE

*"I would like you to try and visualize in your mind's eye, that when you came to school this morning there were no roads, no school buses, no vehicles, no stores, no houses or hospitals. Everything you need to survive: water, food, clothing, shelter, and medicine, you had to get from the forests, fields, creeks, swamps, and rivers. That was the world the Lenape people lived in."*

*-Chitkuwipethakhon (Chief Quiet Thunder)*

## CONTENTS

**ACKNOWLEDGMENTS**

It was my honor and privilege to complete this work. First, I want to thank Marcia Adams, a historian from Delaware who initiated this project. I also am grateful to my friends, Barbara Woolley and Tom Cooper; your enthusiastic support and review of the first draft were invaluable.

I would also like to thank Tom Brown, Jr. at the Tracker School and Malcolm Ringwalt at Earth-Heart Oneness Quest. I sincerely appreciate your inspiring courses and unwavering dedication to the vision and teachings of Grandfather Stalking Wolf. Your training gave me a deeper understanding of our native culture, which brought insight and direction to my discussions with Chief Quiet Thunder.

My deep appreciation goes to Jim Three Buck Gilbert for your extensive knowledge of Indian culture and thoughtful review, as well as Christine Wilson and Dr. Bill Thomas for your manuscript review and comments.

A heartfelt THANK YOU to my friends, Sterling Brown and Dina DeSalvo; I am deeply indebted for your thorough editorial review and supportive writing advice. I want to thank Donna Connor and Bill Horin for your generous help with Adobe Photoshop. Thanks to RuthAnn Purchase for your help with the Lenape maps. Sincere thanks to all my family and friends who expressed an interest in my work on this project.

Finally, I would like to thank my good friend, Chief Quiet Thunder, for sharing your traditional Indian culture with us, for your dedication to protecting our sacred Earth, and your patience, humor, and friendship.

-Greg Vizzi

Note: Certain words and ideas are emphasized because of their significance to the Natural World and indigenous culture. For that purpose, I used italics and set sentences apart from paragraphs. Some words referring to the Natural World are capitalized, respecting the sacredness of the Creation. Words relating to ceremonies are also capitalized.

## INTRODUCTION BY CHIEF QUIET THUNDER

I am fortunate to know many of the traditional ways of the Lenni-Lenape. The name Lenni-Lenape means Original People. For many years I have talked to groups in schools, churches, parks, and other public settings. I decided I wanted to get down in writing the stories and history that I've shared orally over the years. My original goal was to pass on to my children and grandchildren the important spiritual beliefs of their ancestors and help them remember me. If I can also help other people gain a better understanding of the native people of North America, then this book will exceed my goals.

*Mother Earth is the giver of life and the protector of the spirit after life, for all people, not just the Indian people.*

We have a *sacred obligation* to protect the Earth and to learn to live in harmony with the Earth. The Indian people of North America were forced to give up their religion and way of life for many years to the point where much has been lost. I believe the Creator has selected me to express and teach these ideas and ways of life, not only for Indian people, but also for all people willing to listen. I have noticed that people are becoming more receptive. They are seeing that there needs to be more to life and that they can learn by looking at how others have lived on this Earth. In my presentations I try to do more than simply entertain people with colorful outfits and trinkets. I try to pass on ideas that meant something to my family and my ancestors—ideas that still have significance today.

I want to tell my children and others who the Lenape were, how they lived, and what they believed. They were good people, not evil in any way, as some people used to think. This book combines an oral history of my people, their way of life, and their spirituality. It also contains some of my personal life stories and beliefs as a Native American in the modern world. I developed my beliefs through spending time in the wild, talking to elders, and maintaining the traditional ways. Beyond giving my children something to hold onto when I am gone, I want to help keep traditional Indian spirituality alive by teaching Indians who have lost touch with the past as well as non-Indians who can use these ideas to strengthen their own lives in the modern world.

The Lenape believed that each person makes their own spiritual connection and establishes their own spiritual beliefs, using the beliefs of their ancestors as a starting point. People may disagree with some of my beliefs and that is fine. The Indian people still possess the native spirit of this land, and I believe we can help others learn about this spirit, which must not be lost. The Creator meant for Indians to be here. I believe the events that occurred after the Europeans came here happened for reasons only the Creator could understand. While many Indians prefer to keep their culture, traditions, and beliefs secret, sharing only within their tribes, I believe strongly that it is through sharing our rich past that Native Americans can have the greatest positive impact on the modern world. I would like to dedicate this book in honor of my grandmother, Anna Gilbert. *Wanìshi* (thank you) for reading my story.

–Dick Quiet Thunder Gilbert -Chitkuwipethakhon

# 1.
# GROWING UP

*"We do not want riches, but we do want to train our children right."*
*-Red Cloud, Oglala Lakota*

### First Impressions: The Touch of the Wind, the Songs of the Birds

I was born in the town of Woodbury, in southern New Jersey, on June 13, 1934.

My parents and my grandparents were Native American Indians. *We are indigenous to this land.*

The forest surrounding our home was abundant with life. Seeing a hummingbird was one of my very first memories as a child. My grandmother took me outside to our backyard on a sunny spring morning. In that memory, I can feel the cool wind blowing on my face. I look up and see puffy white clouds drifting in a blue sky. The trees and flowers are shaking gently in the wind, especially red trumpet flowers. My eyes focus on the dancing colors. A tiny hummingbird suddenly appears. It dips into a trumpet flower, hovers briefly, and zips to another—I'm captivated by it. With precise bursts, it shifts back and forth: hovering, dipping, feeding, then gone. I look over and see my mother hanging clothes; I watch them blowing in the wind—then the memory fades. I think that was the first time I actually started putting thoughts together.

There was always wildlife around. I saw a lot of birds, squirrels, and rabbits. Another time, I remember hearing baby birds peeping in the backyard. My father had put a birdhouse up in a tree. I knew there were baby birds in it and I watched periodically until they eventually flew out. I can still see them flying out. I had a natural curiosity and fascination with Nature. I lived in an environment that was just made to order for a person like me.

The wind was alive; it was life-giving. I was a person being injected with stimulating sights and sounds, like hearing birds singing the first thing in the morning. *You know, for a kid who was just starting to develop, those sounds were the tunes going on in my head.*

Traditionally, Indian children spent more time with their grandparents, aunts, and uncles than with their parents, because their parents were still growing. That gave the parents a break from child rearing and time to continue their own learning. It also gave the grandparents a sense of knowing they still had an important role to play in the family, rather than being cast aside like they are in modern society. The grandparents' knowledge brought a stabilizing effect to the whole family, and the children learned to respect their elders at an early age. That had been like a stepping stone right down through their aunts and uncles and their parents.

*Our grandparents' knowledge had a lot to do with why our family units were so strong.*

## Natural Medicine and the Good Red Path

I was a skinny little kid growing up. I was quick and fast, but every winter I got pneumonia, and fevers tore me up.

My grandmother Anna, my father's mother, was the one who spent a lot of time with me when I was a small boy growing up. She's the one who helped me through those bad winter bouts with pneumonia. My grandmother made a *Medicine* to help me when I was having that pneumonia so bad. She mixed tobacco and blackstrap molasses together; this was made into a cough syrup. I can still see her crushing it up, adding water, and cooking it into syrup. From what little I can remember, there was something about sulfur in the molasses mixed with the tobacco that brought the phlegm up. I'll never forget that smell; it was a terrible smell, and it started me coughing, but it brought that phlegm up.

I remember a lot about her and one experience in particular. I had to be three or four; I just came through a terrible winter of fevers from pneumonia that stripped me down to skin and bones. It's a vivid memory. On that beautiful spring morning, my grandmother took me by the hand and walked me into a wild strawberry patch. After being closed off from the sun, wind, and fresh air, my senses began to awaken. I could feel the cool breeze on my cheek and sensations of colors, sights, and sounds. She sat me down and said to only eat the red berries. Their sweet taste burst in my mouth. I felt the coolness of the Earth and the wind. I was tasting those sweet berries and watching baby rabbits and box turtles come into the strawberry patch to feed. I looked up and saw fluffy white clouds moving in a beautiful blue sky. Gradually, a powerful feeling came over me. *At that time, I was too young to understand what was taking place, but my grandmother was spiritually connecting me to Mother Earth. She's the one who put my feet in that Good Red Path and I've never left it.*

FRAGARIA VESCA L. ЗЕМЛЯНИКА.

The strawberry is a very special plant; it had a lot of significance, because we had just come through a winter. In my case, I needed that spring fruit because I had been so sick from pneumonia. Those bouts with pneumonia came around mid-winter, and it was a terrible time for me. It was at a time when there was no work and no money. Doctors did not minister to Indian people. Only the grace of the Creator and the fact that my grandmother still remembered the old medicines are what pulled me through. In my fifth winter, I almost died from pneumonia.

*I can still see my grandmother's face, and her hand reaching through the fog, pulling me back from death. She would not let me die.*

She took me many times to gather medicines from the Natural World. I learned early in life what was helping me. It wasn't a drugstore or patent medicine; it was the medicine Mother Earth was producing. It was medicine the Creator had put here. Strawberries are a very powerful plant with a special fruit. It probably has a lot to do with why I am still here today. So, at this time of year I think about strawberries, the medicine in the strawberries, and my grandmother. They are all very fond memories.

All through the rest of the season we had huckleberries, blackberries, raspberries, and currants, which were sour but very appealing. There were various fruits, acorns, nuts, and mushrooms. My grandmother gathered the acorns and all those other foods. She used certain mushrooms to make medicines. I remember she dried them and put them in jars. At certain times of the year, she would crush them up and mix that in with other foods she cooked in the dead of winter. I am surmising that it had something to do with vitamin C and things like that. Unfortunately, I have either forgotten or I never really got a handle on those things.

She had a way about her; she walked very relaxed and confidently. She didn't talk—very little talk, but she had a way of conveying what was on her mind to me. Sometimes it was just a simple gesture of her hand. That was my grandmother. A Ho Ka! (So be it.)

### Grapes and Green Apples

I would climb up an apple tree in the morning and stay there all day. Nobody in the world ate as many green apples as I did. We had a grape arbor that ran from the yard to the back part of the house. It was like a tunnel, and I sometimes started at one end in the morning and ate to the other end. Then I turned around at noontime and ate my way back.

There were a lot of fruit and nut trees around where we lived; we had persimmons, pears, apples, peaches, cherries, and black-heart cherries. I remember eating those persimmons and that sweet taste. I picked the cherries, and my grandmother and sisters made cherry pies in the late fall. I wasn't in school yet, so it was before I was five. One of my functions in the fall was to gather the walnuts from our two walnut trees and remove the shells. In the wintertime, my sisters made "peanut brittle" and fudge with those walnuts. I think being in this type of setting just set the stage for the kind of world I was going to grow up in.

*I learned early in life that the Natural World was supplying all of our water, food, and medicines, so that tied me closer to the land.*

### My English Name: Gilbert

This is the story as it's been told to me. In our family's distant past, somewhere in eastern Virginia, there was a Frenchman who owned a store. He was also the constable, the postmaster, and the minister because he could read and write. His name was Gilebert (probably pronounced something like Jill-Bear). One of my distant grandfathers, a Powhatan Indian, traded furs with Gilebert the Frenchman. Eventually, the authorities wanted to register the names of all the people who lived in the area. When they got to my distant grandfather, no one could pronounce his Indian name. But they wanted to have him on record, so at the store, they put down his name as Gilebert's trapper. Later on, when the English took over that area, instead of calling the Frenchman Gilebert, they called him by the English name: Gilbert. The trapper part eventually got dropped from my great-grandfather's name. So that's how Gilbert became our family name.

That's how it's been told to me by my family members, and I know from talking to other Indian people, it was a common practice. Often, the person who had the pen couldn't speak or pronounce the Indian name, so in many cases, they put down their own name. That's how a lot of Indians wound up with other people's names. Before they knew it, they had a new name, so European names can sometimes throw you off.

### My Indian Name: Quiet Thunder

I have always been fascinated by thunder. When I was growing up I encountered many thunderstorms while fishing and exploring Woodbury Creek. When I heard a low rumble, I knew a storm was coming. Storms always seemed to come up the creek with the tide. I have had some pretty close calls with lightning striking nearby, and sometimes I had to take shelter under the Evergreen Avenue Bridge. I think those experiences gave me a strong connection to thunder.

One time, I heard a storm coming in the distance, so I held my infant daughter quietly in the doorway and listened to the soft rumble of thunder. I didn't want her to be afraid of it. A peaceful feeling came over me as I held her in my arms. The words: *quiet thunder* came into my thoughts. I liked it, and I believe I started using that for my name after giving one of my early presentations at the Rankokus Indian Reservation in New Jersey. I was telling the story of when my grandmother took me out to the strawberry patch. While I was thinking about my grandmother, this name *Quiet Thunder* came into my thoughts again. In the story, I had just gotten over a severe bout with pneumonia and I was anything but thunder. It was as if my grandmother had whispered the name to me. After that, I began using the name, and the media picked up on it. Since then, people have told me that the name reflects the way I speak. The Lenni-Lenape word for Quiet Thunder is *Chitkuwipethakhon.* In our home when I was a kid, we didn't talk a lot about our Indian ancestry. We only had English

names, but we knew who we were. Our past might come up briefly in a conversation, but it wasn't something that was emphasized.

People sometimes ask: "What is the proper way to address you?" I've gotten to this stage in life to not be so sensitive to a name. You can call me a Native American. You can call me an Indian. You can call me a Lenni-Lenape. You can call me Quiet Thunder. You can also call me Dick Gilbert. I am not that sensitive to a thing like this, as long as you don't call me a Delaware, because I am not a Delaware—that was Lord De La War's thing. He was a man with quite an ego. The state of Delaware was named after him, the river and bay were named after him, and the tribe was named after him. I protest being called a Delaware, because I am *not* a Delaware, it gives the impression that we are his children.

We are the Lenni-Lenape people—the Original People of this land and the Grandfather Tribe of the Algonquin people.

## My Family

My mother's name was Carol and her maiden name was Cuff. Her people are Lenni-Lenape from southern New Jersey.

My father's parents, Anna and Harry Gilbert, were Powhatan, from Virginia. My father was young when his father passed away, and he never knew which tribe he descended from because of the displacement of the tribes in the past. They settled in Philadelphia, Pennsylvania. My father's name was also Harry and he had a younger brother, Herman, but we all knew him as Uncle Copper. Now, I don't know who gave him that nickname, but it had something to do with how he could strike you so fast—like a copperhead snake.

My father and Uncle Copper grew up in Philadelphia, and after their father died, my grandmother took in washing, ironing, and things like that. They lived in a predominantly Irish neighborhood as small boys. My father was the oldest. He said Copper wouldn't fight. Those Irish kids picked on him, and my father had to take the fight for him. Well, that went on for so long, and then my father made Copper fight. Once he fought back, he realized it wasn't so bad. He kind of liked it; so I think that's where the name Copper came in—he could strike you fast.

My mother was born and grew up at her family's homestead in Gouldtown, New Jersey, where their Lenape village had been. Many Lenape Indians never left New Jersey. In the past, they blended in to survive. We were living in a circumstance where we were surrounded by the dominant society. My family did not talk about our Indian past because we had to function in this modern world. *To my family, the Indian thing had come and gone.*

After my mother and father married, my father moved to the homestead in Gouldtown. I had four older brothers and three older sisters, so I am the baby of the family. They were all born at home in Gouldtown, except for my oldest sister who was born in Woodbury.

After my father's father passed away, my grandmother married Doctor Goodbreed. He was an interesting individual: a man of color, originally from Georgia. He was a good doctor. He was not a bona fide medical doctor, but an herbal doctor. He died before I was born. I remember one type of medicine when I was growing up that had a picture of an Indian on the pill package. He couldn't get a patent because he was colored. There was a Jewish pharmacist in Philadelphia who had it patented under his name with the understanding that the proceeds would go to Dr. Goodbreed. At his death, the patent would go to the Jewish pharmacist, and as far as I know, it did.

We eventually moved to Dr. Goodbreed's property in Woodbury. We all lived under one roof at the end of Dickerson Street, a one-lane dirt road that ran through the woods and led up to the main street of Woodbury. Do you remember that TV show, *The Waltons*? My family was very much like that when I was growing up. There was my mother and father, my father's mother, my four brothers, two sisters, Uncle Copper, and me. My sister Ethel was the oldest; she was close to 90 years old when she passed away in 2007. Then there is Anna, Catherine, Harry (who passed away in 2007), Herman (who passed in 2011), Ralph, Jim Three Buck, and me. My two brothers and one of my sisters live in New Jersey, within a half an hour of each other. One sister lives in Orlando, Florida.

**Family Pictures**

There were not a lot of pictures in the home when I was growing up. I can only come to the conclusion that it was an expense. We did not have the luxury of having the money to do that, but we did have some pictures. I have two pictures that are part of my ancestry from the past; they are good copies of both my grandmothers.

The first one is a picture of my mother's mother, Annie. I never knew her. I think it's the only picture of her that we have. I was told she was a very nice looking woman: tall, broad shouldered, slender. In the picture, she's wearing her hair in the Indian style with two braids. The woods are in the background. This picture was taken in Gouldtown on Buckshutem Road about 300 yards from Five Points; that's where five trails came together. That area was where my mother's people had their village.

The other picture is my grandmother, Anna, from my father's side. There was a portrait of her that hung in the living room of the homestead for years. In that picture she looked like Geronimo. If you looked at her and did not know she was a woman and just looked at her face, she looked like the image of Geronimo. Sad to say, I have no picture of my Uncle Copper, and the one I have of my father isn't a very good one; you can't distinguish him too much.

**My Heroes**

My heroes were my father, my Uncle Copper, and my four brothers. As a boy growing up, I learned a lot from my four older brothers about fishing, trapping, hunting, and relating to Nature, because I was outdoors practically every day. I could apply everything I learned from my heroes almost on a daily basis. During the Depression years, I was still pretty young.

I learned from my grandmother about gathering the medicines and wild fruits. A little bit later in life, my older brothers taught me how to trap the different animals and how to fish and hunt. Many times when I was healthy enough, I tagged along with them when they went fishing or trapping.

*I realized at an early age that my brothers supplied most of the meat that was put on the table, so the land is what pulled us through during those tough times.*

I was eager to be old enough to be able to go and do the same things. After learning to set traps and snares, I learned to use a shotgun. I hunted rabbits, squirrels, possum, pheasants, and quail, and I trapped muskrats. The night before hunting season opened I was up all night checking my shells, and I guess I oiled my gun a hundred times. I was excited, and I am still that way. I spent a lot more time with my brothers Ralph and Jim because they were closer to my age.

When we camped, sometimes we packed a whole bird in clay and then put that in the fire and ashes, which baked the bird. Then, when we broke away the clay, the feathers and everything came off. It was a very easy way to acquire meat. We hunted as a family. My two oldest brothers had learned from my father and my uncle, so it was like fulfilling a common destiny. Now it was *my* turn, and I was fully prepared. By spending so much time in the woods, I knew pretty much where all the game was. I knew where the animals would be at certain times of the day and in different seasons, and weather patterns. So I became a better-than-average hunter. I loved it; I felt like this is what my life was supposed to be.

It was a big event when we came back from hunting. After hunting either ducks or rabbits, I remember Mom asking, "Did you get anything, boys?" And before I was old enough to hunt, when my older brothers came back from the hunt, I remember my grandmother asking the very same thing: "Did you get anything, boys?" As I got older, I read about the Indian people of the past and how it was a big event when the hunter came home with game. You know, for a young kid to be able to be a part of that—I can imagine how Indian people felt way, way back. I missed my time by about 500 years.

**Setting a Trap**

As a young boy, I hunted with bows and arrows, stones, and traps. I traveled with my brother Jim, who is next to me in age, and my brother Ralph, who was next to him. They taught me how to make deadfall traps and where to set them for different animals. A deadfall is a type of trap with either a large rock or log that comes down and instantly kills the animal. It has a trigger. The trigger was originally called a Paiute trigger because they thought it was the Paiute Indians who first came up with this idea. It's in the shape of a figure 4. Today it is called a figure-4 trigger. You can have a small deadfall trap for an animal like a mouse or a squirrel, or you can build them large enough to kill a bear. I had 12 of those traps around Woodbury Creek where I hunted, fished, and trapped. I had to check those traps twice a day: once in the morning and again in the evening.

They are excellent traps. To set one properly you put a brush pile or a rock pile around it and have the opening on one side so that the animal will go after the bait in the direction you want it to. They will follow the course of least resistance. When this trap comes down, it comes down so fast and heavy, the animal is killed instantly. They don't suffer compared to many of the modern metal traps that will trap the animal but hold it in captivity until the trapper comes and dispatches it.

You determine what type of animal you will draw by the kind of bait you use. For something like a squirrel or a little bigger animal, we used acorns, corn, or some type of seed. Now, if you were after a raccoon or a possum, you used fish: something that had flesh. The figure-4 deadfall trap is designed so that when the animal tries to pull the bait off the stick, it causes the figure-4 to collapse, bringing the whole structure down. The figure-4 is the trigger; the part that comes down on the animal is the deadfall. It really is simple, but works very well. Do you know the expression "caught between a rock and a hard place?" That goes back to ancient times, referring to the deadfall trap.

The snare uses a sapling, which is bent over. It is very springy and is tied to a rope or a cord with a loop on the end. You set this up so the loop is suspended off the ground, and the bait is put in the middle. It is designed so that when the animal puts its head inside the loop, it causes the triggers to go off. The sapling springs up, tightens the noose around the animal's neck, and yanks the animal off the ground, killing it quickly. It supplied quite a lot of meat when I was a young boy coming along.

### Let's Go Fishing

I was very content to spend my days down at the creek wading in at low tide to catch fish. One of my favorite ways to catch fish was to use a tree sapling for a fish snare. Instead of the snare having a noose, it has a little sliver of deer leg bone for a hook. The bone is rubbed on a braiding stone to get sharp points on both ends to put the worm on. This "hook" is tied to a trigger with a line. The line is attached to the sapling, and the trigger is set into a wood stake that's hammered into the creek bank. You toss this out into the creek, and the catfish comes along and swallows the worm with the "hook," which goes down in the fish's belly. Then, as the fish swims away, he starts jerking to try to get loose and causes this trigger to open—so the sapling flies up and pulls the fish out of the water. You have it arranged so that it holds him high enough out of the water so the snappers and the raccoons can't get him.

The good thing about this type of snare is that you can set it and leave; you don't have to stay there. I observed my brothers Ralph and Jim make those snares. The first time I set one, my anticipation was intense. That kind of anticipation I don't have the words for; it was just exciting. This is the day that I find out: is it going to work, am I capable of making it work, will it bear fruit? The first fish I caught in my snare was a catfish. It felt great. It was a real sense of accomplishment that I could do something that nobody in the world could do besides my brothers.

*It made me feel very responsible, and it was rewarding that I could contribute food to the table. I believe that played a part in bringing my "Indianism" to the surface.*

You see, in my world back then, nobody was into these things. There were no kids I knew of who came into that Woodbury Creek environment. Much later, I set 12 of those snares along Woodbury Creek. In the morning, I walked down to the bank to see which snares had catfish. I took my knife, because I had to use a knife to get the bone out. I'd open him up and take the bone out, then put another worm on and toss it back in for the day's fishing. That evening just before dark, I'd go back to check and see which ones had fish, take them off, put on a worm, and do a little night fishing.

*That's how I was able to supply fish for the family at nine years old.*

### The Family Unit

In the past, you had a responsibility to your family. You started when you were very small, and you had certain tasks that you did, like in the fishing story. I'd be sitting in the kitchen watching my older sisters, mother, or grandmother preparing the fish. I felt pretty big because I knew I helped to put those fish there.

*All these events may seem little, but in the overall scheme of things they are big. They are what tied us close to our family. This is how you build strength with your family at a very early age, by contributing and learning.*

I knew that whatever my older brothers and sisters learned, they would pass on to me. It builds a strength and cohesiveness that is definitely missing today. The earlier you start, the better. Families are really under duress today because we are not functioning as families. The kids are left to watch TV or whatever it might be, and there is not much interaction as family units. It's creating problems.

## The Land Provided for Us

*What was emphasized was how to survive off the land, especially during those Depression years when conditions were tough.*

We grew our own vegetables and fruit. We hunted, trapped, and fished for our meat. Corn, squash, and beans were staples. Traditionally, almost every meal had some form of corn. One popular meal with corn and beans is succotash. Making it the old way, fish heads are used for the meat portion. There is a lot of meat on a fish head, and it helps season the dish. Since those were the staples, it was very important for every village or family group who had a garden to grow those crops. Anything left over from the fish that we didn't eat was put into the garden for fertilizer.

Just as we used every part of the fish, we used every part of the deer. Even the undigested food in the deer's stomach was used as a poultice to heal a boil or other infections. The brains were used in the processing of the hides. The bones were all used for various tools. *No part of that animal was excluded.*

## Keeping Memories Alive

One of our family traditions was to plant a tree to commemorate a special occasion. Anytime there was a birth, a holiday, or special event, my family planted a tree around where we lived, so we had plenty of pine and cedar trees. When we brought a Christmas tree inside, we brought it in with the roots and everything. Then it was replanted outside after the holiday. My family planned ahead because the winters back then were real winters. The ground was frozen, but they already had that hole dug before the winter freeze came. That was the way they thought. Why kill a living tree unnecessarily? In this case, it became part of the history of the children and the family itself. Those were the trees I remember the most. I also remember the wild cherry trees where the tent caterpillars built their webs. We burned the nest right after dark when all the caterpillars came back for the night. I don't remember any other thing that caused a problem with our trees.

## Discipline

I can only remember my father whipping me one time. That was a serious situation. I was still kind of small. There was an abandoned house up the road from where we lived. The house had been boarded up for as long as I can remember. There was a field of Indian grass on the side of this house. I was out there and I had set that field on fire; I was going to burn out the settlers. Just as it happened, my father came walking down the road. I took off and ran back into the kitchen, down the hall, and hid under the bed. It took him a while to put that fire out.

I heard him come in the kitchen and ask my grandmother, "Where is he at?"

She said, "He's under the bed."

He used a razor strap. That was the only time he ever whipped me, but brother! We used to wear those long drawers. They only came down to your knees, and they had the buttons and flap in the back.

He said, "Unbutton your flap," and boy, did he lay that razor strap on me! I put my hand close to my butt and could feel the heat like a blowtorch. I never forgot that, and he never had to do it again.

Usually, he just looked at me, and if that didn't get it, he would say, "Boy, do you know what you are doing?" That meant I had better get my act together.

He was uncanny. Sunday morning breakfast was a big thing with us. One Sunday morning, I was sitting there, and in my mind I was going to sneak the shotgun out of the house, through the woods, and shoot some squirrels at the creek. I had never done this before.

He looked across the kitchen table and said, "Boy, I don't want you going out of this house with that gun today." How he knew that I will never know. After that, I wouldn't even think about certain things—or else!

Back then, my father made his living digging wells, but in the wintertime, he made money off the woods. He cut firewood and made axe and hoe handles. I can remember watching my father and Uncle Copper in the backyard making those handles. That last bit of work was always done with a fine piece of glass. It was quite a finished work. Some of the older people said that no self-respecting gardener or woodsman would be caught with an axe or a hoe with a handle that wasn't made by the Gilbert brothers.

## The Five Whites

Uncle Copper didn't do a lot of talking; he had a serious demeanor. When he spoke to you, you knew he was going to tell you something important, like knowledge that would benefit you. The implication was: Listen to what I'm going to tell you and digest it, because it can save you a lot of agony. He wouldn't elaborate; he made a statement and that was it—it wasn't explained to you. When we turned 13 or 14, it was our Uncle Copper's responsibility to have a little sit-down talk with each boy.

When it was my turn, he said, "There is something I want to talk to you about." I felt anxious, but I was excited to hear his message. We sat down in the backyard and he told me about the five whites. Now, I hope this does not offend anyone, but he said, "Always avoid the five whites: white sugar, white flour, white salt, white whiskey, and white women. They are all incompatible to the Indian man."

After I told my son, Vince, about the five whites, he said, "Dad, I can go along with all that, except for the white women." Vince married a white woman.

## I Was Different

I believe I was different because of one thing: I took to the outdoors in a big way; that's where I really felt at home.

There was a huge gravel hole near the neighborhood, and everybody in the community learned how to swim in it. The community considered me kind of a strange kid. If a storm was coming and everybody else went running for cover, I stayed there in the gravel hole because nobody was there; I had it all to myself. If a snowstorm was coming and everybody was rushing to get home, that's when I wanted to be in the woods. I wanted to see what takes place. I wanted to be a part of what Nature is. Running and hiding from a storm? That didn't seem right to me. If I am a person who is a part of Nature, I have to know what Nature is all about; not just in its beautiful times when the sun is shining, but when the weather is at its severest. I think it strengthened me physically—I know it has mentally. I felt very comfortable out in the woods, swamps, and creeks. I wanted to absorb everything around me. Others were not able to relate to that world, so I preferred to be alone. That's one of the reasons why I was considered a strange little kid. The other kids were out playing baseball, and I was heading for the swamps.

Back when I was growing up, in our particular area, the land filtered the water and was not polluted. When I went into the forests and swamps I didn't see houses or hear cars. It was like stepping back in time. On occasion, my Indian past would come to the surface. When it happened, I was alone, and it was very personal. At the creek bank, I sometimes imagined the Indians of old walking those trails along the creek, or stopping to get a drink of water. To me, it seemed pristine, like it was in the past. The water in those streams was crystal clear and good to drink.

There was a great abundance of animals where we hunted, fished, and trapped. Spatterdock, a type of water lily, was plentiful. It was used by my ancestors as a food source. The meadows were filled with wild rice. There were no phragmites (invasive reeds). It was one of the greatest feelings—that I was in an environment untouched by man. The only signs of disturbance from man were the old Indian trails along the creeks.

*I know those early years had quite a bearing on who I am today.*

## The Great Pretender

Now a little humor. What the local people called sand vipers were actually eastern hognose snakes. The locals thought those snakes were poisonous. They're called "The Great Pretender" because they act and look just like a poisonous snake; they hiss and flatten their necks like a cobra ready to strike. When I was a kid, there were a lot of frogs and hop toads all around the creeks, swamps, ponds, and gravel pits, which meant a lot of snakes. My brother Ralph taught me how to identify and handle the snakes in our area without getting bitten. So I didn't have any fear of snakes as I wandered the forests and wetlands. When I did find a hognose snake, I knew how to catch it. If I saw somebody near one of my favorite places in a swamp or the gravel hole, I'd catch one of those snakes. Then I'd bring it to Steven's Convenience Store where the neighborhood kids hung out.

Everybody was afraid of snakes, and they'd say, "Where did you get that snake?" I'd

say, "Oh, I got it down there by the spring." Well, I knew I would not have to worry about anyone coming around the spring that summer! I laugh about it now.

Hognose snakes are becoming rare. I think the last one I saw over in that part of New Jersey was in the late 1950s. As the area started to build up, the snakes began to disappear. So my wanderings put me a little bit out of touch with the community and probably even with some of my own family. *But it put me in touch with who I am, and it stayed with me.* That's the one thing I believe that has kept me on this track. The rest of the family sought to be like the dominant society; I sought isolation. I would much rather go down to the creek and spend my entire day there alone, or go into the swamps, than to be around other people.

I love to go back to all those peaceful days I spent by the creek and in the woods exploring the Natural World and watching the animal life. *It was paradise to me.*

## I Wouldn't Trade My Childhood

Today, a section of Woodbury Creek has been dammed up, and it's become Stuart Lake. When I was a kid, the high ground where they built the Gloucester County YMCA was all woods, fields, and meadows; there wasn't anything else around. I took Brian, my oldest grandson, there some years ago and described the landscape to him—how it was when I was a boy.

If you walk down the hill from the YMCA, you will see a little boat ramp on the lake. About fifty yards out from the ramp, in the mud, there is a V-shaped stone trap. It's a fish trap that my brothers and I built back in the late 1940s. Back then, if you looked straight across from where the boat ramp is today, you would have seen 12 tulip poplar tree saplings along the far bank. They were planted by my father. We used those saplings for fish snares. That was over 70 years ago. When I was nine years old, I used them every day. They all grew to be tall trees before they were cut down.

I couldn't have asked for a better childhood. I was out of the house at sunup, and I didn't come back until dark. I roamed the swamps, creeks, and woods; I discovered red salamanders, shrews, all kinds of snakes, frogs, and turtles, and had many wondrous experiences. I have a very limited formal education, but I think I have a very good knowledge of Nature and how to live in balance with the Natural World.

*I spent most of my childhood in the woods; I was at the creek practically every day. I grew up with the changing of the tides and the seasons.*

That area really hadn't changed much, I believe, in hundreds of years. It didn't start changing until the Second World War came about, and then—boy did it change!

I wouldn't trade my childhood.

# 2.
# IN THE BEGINNING: AN INTRODUCTION TO THE PEOPLE

*"I am Indian, and my aim, my joy, and my pride is to sing the glories of my own people. My concern is to rekindle the ancestral fires of Hope and Inspiration within their own circles." -Chief Quiet Thunder*

### The Turtle and the Red Cedar Tree

In our mythology of the creation of this land, which we call *Turtle Island:*

> *The Creator first created Grandfather Sky, and later, the Waters. It was like that for a very long time. Then, a Giant Turtle surfaced, and the Water ran off the Turtle's back. Then later, the first Red Cedar Tree grew up from the Turtle's back. The first Lenape Man and Woman came from the roots of that Great Red Cedar Tree.*

That's why the red cedar is sacred to traditional Lenape people. The turtle is also a very sacred symbol to us. The snapping turtle, in my understanding, is the turtle that represents this Turtle Island: North America. The turtle also represents the Mother Earth, fertility, and long life. This mythology of the creation of this land we call Turtle Island is not just with the Lenape; many tribes have the same mythology.

*Turtle Island is made up of the blood, the flesh, and the bones of thousands of years of my ancestors who have died and gone back to Mother Earth.*

Our religion tells us we come from Mother Earth and we are to return to Mother Earth. In our way of life, Nature is all powerful for one reason: it provides everything that we need. Because of this very close connection, we have a *sacred obligation* to protect this land. This land consists of the spirits of my ancestors. We are the indigenous people of this land. We have always been here.

*We are tied to this land because of this ancestral way and our original religion that was based on the Creation.*

## The Grandfather Tribe

Lenni-Lenape means Original People. Not in the sense of Adam and Eve, but if you go north into Nova Scotia, or parts of Canada and Maine, talk to the Micmac or Passamaquoddy. Ask them, "Who was the Grandfather Tribe?" If you travel along the Great Lakes, ask the Ojibwa and Chippewa. Go into the southeastern states and ask the Nanticokes, the Choptanks (what few you can still find), the Piscataways, and the Conoys. If you seek out those elders, and most of all, the Algonquin-speaking people who still remember the old traditional ways, and ask them, "Who was the Grandfather Tribe?" they will tell you it was the Lenni-Lenape.

In the early days of tribal expansion, as a village started to get overpopulated and put too much pressure on resources, some families moved away to a new area. Those families grew to become the various Algonquin tribes. Eventually, the lands of the Lenape extended widely throughout the Northeast. The size of the tribe determined the size of the area they occupied. Sometimes they took the name of a dominant feature in Nature such as a river, a lake, or mountain. Nanticoke means Tidewater People because they live near the tidal waters. Other tribes may give them a name that is different from their own name.

I think some of the Indians along the Great Lakes area referred to the Lakota Sioux as "cutthroats" because in warfare they would supposedly cut your throat. The Nez Perce bred the Appaloosa horse. Another tribe that traded horses with them may name them something that deals with horses. So it varies from tribe to tribe. But usually, names are based on geographical features in the lands where they lived. Some of the western tribes referred to the Lenni-Lenape as *The Morning Sunrise People*, because we were the first to greet the sun. The Algonquin people are all related to the Lenni-Lenape. We are all brothers and sisters and cousins, but we were the earliest tribe in the East. That is why Lenni-Lenape means Original People.

### Who's In Charge?

In the past, the Clan Mothers were the principle power behind the selection of a Lenape chief. My understanding is that they selected chiefs on their merit, their ability to make good decisions, and their generosity. The final decision was made by mutual consent within the tribal council, but the Clan Mothers carried a lot of influence in the selection of a chief. Originally, if someone had been elected a chief, he remained a chief all his life. With some tribes, if a new chief was elected, the old chief would lose his status. With others, he would keep it. In the case of my tribe, I am still considered a chief.

There are some tribes where, if the father was a chief, the son automatically became the chief. That doesn't fit in with my understanding of Lenape culture. It should be the people who decide if someone is a chief or not, because I know the way the people thought: they looked for qualities of good judgement and generosity and putting the people first. A hereditary chief might not fulfill these requirements. A Lenape chief can be either a man or a woman; that was the case in the past, as well as today. Currently, the tribal council normally handles disputes. Sometimes they might appoint committees for specific duties, disputes or programs. The council usually has the final say.

### Do All Indians Look Alike?

Tribes from different locations have different physical attributes. A lot of that depends upon the geographical conditions where they lived. Take the Plains Indians, the Sioux in particular. They were out in the open where the wind and the sun had a big effect on them. You will notice that their cheekbones are pretty high, and they have the very prominent aquiline nose. Their skin generally is darker, and their hair is dark and coarse. They are deep-chested, with eyes set deep in. They are a very strong, well-built, broad-shouldered people. A lot of that is based on the elements. It is also based on their food source, which was primarily buffalo (North American bison). The buffalo was the dominant animal in their lives, and that animal supplied just about everything they needed. So that animal became the center of their world. It was sacred to them because it was the animal that made it possible for them to exist.

In the East, my people had quite a varied diet. We ate fish, deer, and all types of plant food. The Lenape were generally fairly tall, broad-shouldered, and strong, with dark eyes and straight black hair. We were not, generally speaking, as big, broad-shouldered, and deep-chested, with high cheekbones, and deep set eyes like the Plains Indians. Our environment and what we ate had a different effect on us. We had the forest for shade, so our eyes are more open and skin lighter colored than Indians who were in the sun constantly, such as the Plains Indians or the Apaches. The younger men often shaved both sides of their scalp, leaving a narrow strip of hair along the center of their heads. Bear grease was applied to stiffen it, and an eagle feather was attached. The men shaved with a sharp piece of clam shell or pulled out their hairs to form the hair strip. Because facial hair was considered unmanly, Indians seldom grew beards. Tattoos were common among both the men and the women.

Now, if you look at the Inuit, especially their eyes and cheekbones, you will notice that their cheekbones are very high and their eyes are small. This is due to the influence of the sun glare off the snow and ice. They also developed certain characteristics because of the food they ate. When I was in the workforce, I met a young guy who married a woman from Formosa (Taiwan). Referring to his wife's indigenous people, he said, "Dick, those people look like Plains Indians, they also dress like Plains Indians, and their culture is almost identical." I wasn't aware of it. Well, that set my head to thinking about the theory of the land bridge from Siberia. If you look at the Northwest Indians from up above Seattle and into parts of Canada, the Aleuts and Inuit further north and into the Arctic, you will see they have more of the Asian features. Now, my feeling on this is that they were the last to come across that land bridge on the Bering Straits, so the Asian influence is still very much with them. So much of the way they look at life is similar. The tipi is round and the igloo is round. They see life in cycles, like we do. Prior to the land bridge disappearing, I believe that some people did come across and filtered into other parts of the land, so you will find more of the Asian influence.

*I have been taught by the elders that we have always been here.*

The elders told us that the Creator placed the Europeans in Europe, the Africans in Africa, the Asians in Asia, and the Indians were placed here upon the turtle's back (North America). Scholars and archaeologists claim that everyone here is an immigrant; they believed this land was originally vacant. Why would the Creator leave a whole continent without people?

## A Natural Lifestyle

Meat and fish were a part of our diet, as were vegetables, nuts, fruit, roots, and herbs. It was a varied diet, and from everything I can gather it was an exceptionally healthy diet. The Lenape were a very robust people. They lived outdoors most of their lives, and they wore few clothes so their bodies could breathe, except during very harsh winters. In the summer, a man wore a belt, breechcloth, and moccasins. In colder weather, he attached buckskin leggings to his belt, and in bitter cold he would wear a buckskin vest, shirt, or a coat made with a fur hide from a bear or deer. His coat could also be made up of smaller fur-bearing animal hides. The Lenape women dressed in deerskin skirts that reached their knees and wore their hair in long braids. Like the men, they also wore leggings and moccasins in the winter. In the cold winter, women kept their breasts covered with a shawl of animal fur or feathers.

Before European contact, there were no chemicals and no alcohol or anything that did not go with the natural functions of the body. The Lenape were an exceptionally healthy people, not just because of their diet, but also because of their beliefs. They believed they were a part of Nature—a part of that naturalness, and spiritually connected to the Natural World. I think that tended to make them not just physically exceptional, but also mentally exceptional. *They were in a natural function, not set apart from Nature.*

## Truth is Sacred

The Lenape were a people who had exceptional character—like being truthful.

*When Indians sat down to negotiate a treaty with the Europeans, it was out in the open, under the sun, the sky, the clouds, the birds, the trees, the animals, the land, and all of Creation—all were considered to be sacred.*

Everyone agreed to the conditions of the treaty. When the Europeans broke those agreements, they weren't just breaking their word with the people. From the Indians' standpoint, they were breaking that covenant with the Creator because that agreement was made out in the open under the sky. The Creator was all around, and to break that covenant with the Creator was certain death. That was like a person who, in a Christian view, was certainly going to Hell.

So growing up with that truthfulness, to always tell the truth, is something the Indian people had passed down over the generations. *This was a principle they understood to be the right way to live because it protected everyone.* Nature is *truth,* and that is what the Indians patterned themselves after; Nature was their teacher. The Lenape were taught from a young age that to lie was like committing a sin and carried the severest punishment. I will speak about that later.

## Gatherings

Gatherings gave young people from other families a chance to meet each other, and sometimes marry into other tribes. That helped to keep our bloodlines strong. There didn't always have to be a significant reason, just like how people will go visit relatives, they just wanted to come together. Other times, it would just be friends and relatives (not always from the same tribe) who came together. Gatherings sometimes were for specific reasons, such as weddings, funerals, or someone held in high esteem who became very ill or was dying. Powwows are a time for gathering in a cultural setting where young people can meet. The Lenape Tribe was highly regarded by all the Algonquin people and it was desirable to marry into the Lenape Tribe. With many of those marriages, our influence travelled far and wide.

Today, gatherings are when the people come together for name-giving ceremonies, powwows, or just to be with friends and relatives. They are still especially important for bringing young people together.

**Nations, Tribes, Clans, and Bands**

The nation is the Lenape Nation. In the past, within that nation there were three separate tribes: the Turkey, the Wolf, and the Turtle. The Turkey is the Unalachtigo. The Wolf is the Munsee (or Minsi) tribe. The Unami is the Turtle, which is my tribe. The basic breakdown is the three tribes and then the clans. The tribe is the larger group, which usually has a council and a chief. Generally, a tribe consists of different clans. Your clan is based on your common ancestry: your family. That is your bloodline (see page 126). This is a simple description because much knowledge about the clans has been lost since the upheavals after European contact. But we know the clan system was designed to prevent intermarriage within families, and it also had other functions. These functions included the selection of a tribal chief, and sending out the Peace Chiefs to avoid conflicts. The Clan Mothers worked with them all to facilitate better communication to fulfill their common goals.

A band may consist of people from the different tribes and clans. There may be a band that consists of the Turtle, the Turkey, and the Wolf Clans. A band was just people who came together for common causes, or in some cases, family relationships. Sometimes, the people in a band settled in one place, which would then become a village.

When the American Indian Movement swept across the land in the early 1970s, many of us came out of the shadows and reorganized our tribes. Today, our government-sanctioned name is The Nanticoke Lenni-Lenape Tribal Nation of New Jersey, which is a confederation. It consists of Nanticoke and Lenape Indians from New Jersey and Delaware.

## Bloodlines

People cannot intermarry within a clan. That's how we kept our bloodlines from getting too close. Some years back, I was doing a program for our powwow over in New Jersey. That Saturday morning I was setting up my display and a young Piscataway boy from lower Maryland came over. I guess he was about 19 years old, a very respectful young man. We were talking and I noticed he kept looking at the different clan symbols that I had displayed. He asked me what my clan was and I told him. I could almost guess what his next question was going to be: "Do you have any children?"

I told him, "Yes, I have a son and a daughter." He is of the Turkey Clan and I am of the Turtle, so those two clans can marry. I could see quite a smile on his face until I told him my daughter was only eight years old. This is a serious issue today because over the years so much knowledge of our bloodlines has been lost.

Many Indian people here in the East really don't know what clan they belong to. Marriage to someone of a different clan is a good thing because it keeps the bloodline strong and makes the two clans more closely connected. In the recent past, in order to survive, the people have had to marry outside of their tribes. They married non-Indian people in many cases. The reservation Indians generally, and the Sioux in particular, (in the western part of the country) have a bloodline that is stronger than here in the East with the non-reservation Indians.

One of the ways some of us have kept our bloodlines alive is by New Jersey Indians marrying Indians from Delaware and vice versa. I would say a quarter of the Indian population in New Jersey has married Indian people from Delaware. There is also a lot of mixed blood: some are Indian, some are mixed Indian and white, and some are mixed Indian and black, while some are all three. But now, as the tribes have started to come together, members are accepted into the tribal membership according to their family affiliation. Their bloodlines can be traced back to the original Lenape families by their English names. The elders kept track of who they were over the generations and tried to pass that information on.

## Mixed Blood

One of the things that people ask me is how much Indian blood I have. I can only trace my bloodline as far back as my grandparents and their parents: beyond that, I have no knowledge. There were so many circumstances in the past no one knows about. No one really knows how much Indian blood they have.

Because of the circumstances today, there are Native Americans who some people might say: "They don't look like Indians to me; they look like they are white."

So there are some Indians who have Caucasian features, but they also have an Indian background and bloodline, too. So you can't say well, they're not Indian just because they don't look like that Plains Indian with the high cheekbones and the dark deep-set eyes. Because they are mixed-blood does not mean that they are not Indian. I am sure almost everyone can understand that Indian people found themselves in situations where, if they did not marry outside of their group, there was a strong possibility of breeding themselves into obscurity. That is one of the reasons for the clan system.

Now that the tribes are coming together after all those years, most of them have forgotten who they are clan-wise. Most people here in the East don't really know what I am talking about. So I say that to say this: don't always go by what you think you see. They may very well be more Indian than a lot of people think. It's not just physical attributes. A lot of times it's also what's in your heart.

Now, a little humor. A while back, I went to my doctor for a checkup and he was not in, so I saw another doctor whom I had never met before. Anyway, we got to talking and somehow the subject got around to age.

He asked me my age and I said, "Seventy years old."

He said, "Holy cow, you're not 70!"

I said, "Yes, I am" and I showed him my driver's license.

He said, "That's incredible!" and he called the nurse in and he called the receptionist in and he said, "Now tell the truth, how old do you think this guy is?" One said 56, and they were all very complimentary.

"This guy is 70 years old—look at his body!"

So the receptionist said, "What's your secret?"

I laughed and said, "It's in the blood. I'll sell you a couple of pints."

I am very proud of this Indian blood; it's what makes me who I am. But I don't wrestle with a person because they are half Indian and half white, or half Indian and half black. I maintain this: we are all one race of human beings. It's not necessarily the blood; it's the culture. You are tied into whatever culture you practice. You're an American, that's the first thing—that's number one on the hit parade—you are an American.

*"Thy mind is made straight; thy head is now combed; the seven crooks have been taken from thy body: Now, thou too hast a New Mind."*
*-Deganawida (The Great Peacemaker)*

## Indian Roots of the Constitution

The Iroquois people, also known as the Haudenosaunee or the People of the Longhouse, formed the Six Nations in the state of New York (circa 1142, prior to major European contact). Before that time, the Iroquois people fought amongst themselves, had warrior societies, and were annihilating each other. Then a prophet came down from the North and brought them to peace. He was known as The Great Peacemaker. He and Hiawatha formed the confederation called the Six Nations, or the Iroquois Confederacy. Originally, there were five: the Mohawk, the Seneca, the Cayuga, the Oneida, and the Onondagas.

Prior to Andrew Jackson, there was a lot of conflict in the southern states with white settlers overrunning Indian homelands. The Tuscaroras came up out of the Carolinas on the Appalachian Trail to get away from that conflict. The five nations took them in as the sixth nation. The Tuscaroras were a member of that confederation, but at the time they had no voting rights. The Appalachian Trail was known as the Indian Turnpike, because it was used for travel from one region to another. The United States government is a system partially based on the Iroquois Confederacy. Benjamin Franklin made a statement once:

*"Those so-called 'ignorant savages' can have such a workable system, that we, as civilized Christian people, should be able to do the same thing."*

The U.S. constitution was inspired by the principles of the Iroquois Confederacy. It was the model the founding fathers used to form the Republic. Today we are living under some of the same principles that the Indians in the Iroquois Confederacy live by, for instance, every tribe in that confederation was represented. That's a very brief story of the Six Nations.

## Keeping the Peace

Some history books give the impression there were a lot of conflicts among the Eastern Woodland Indians. This is not true.

Before European contact, there were wars and conflicts among the Iroquois people until the Great Peace and the formation of the Iroquois Confederacy. Many Woodland tribes married into the Lenape, which made them all relatives. The Lenape Tribe was highly regarded among all the Algonquin people, which made it desirable to marry into the Lenape Tribe, and many Algonquins did. With these marriages, the Lenape influence traveled to many of the Algonquin and other tribes, such as the Shawnee in particular, Ojibway, and Chippewa. Not only were the Lenape welcomed in most Woodland villages, they often had relatives there through those marriages. Most of the Northeastern Woodland tribes were peaceful. *Keeping the peace was everyone's responsibility.* First off, we avoided things that could create conflict. If there was conflict, anyone who was close by stepped in, especially if it looked like it could become violent. Family members used peer pressure to maintain fairness and a peaceful family life, but whenever there was a conflict among relatives, they always intervened. It wasn't a materialistic society like we have today. Back then, generosity was valued rather than material possessions and wealth. This accumulation of wealth breeds conflict, like jealousy, and one person looking down on another because he has a lower material status.

Whenever there were conflicts among the tribes, the tribal councils of both tribes sent for the Peace Chiefs. Their responsibility was to sit down with each tribe and try to resolve those situations before they developed into warfare, and usually they could. The Peace Chiefs were clear-thinking individuals who were able to resolve conflicts relatively quickly so they didn't become full-blown wars. Part of the reason there were few conflicts was the great abundance of fish, game, and many other resources—plenty for all. When there was a conflict, it was usually because a tribe had violated another tribe's hunting and fishing areas. The size of the hunting and fishing areas depended upon the size of the tribe. As the tribe grew in population, it needed more hunting and fishing areas. This required some adjustment between the tribes. The key to resolving any disputes was the influence of the Clan Mothers and their Peace Chiefs. By being the Grandfather Tribe, the Lenape were highly thought of, and the people could stand by their decisions because they were well respected. That's why this whole Eastern Seaboard was peaceful. The Peace Chiefs also helped other tribes dispel conflicts, since many of those other tribes were related to the Lenape.

As far back as my oral history goes, prior to European contact, my people did not fight a war. We were a peaceful people; we made no weapons of war. If we were attacked, the hunting bow would become a weapon, the fish spear would become a weapon, the stone knife or hatchet would become a weapon. We never really made weapons of war, that didn't enter into it. It was only after European contact that serious conflicts started. There were interior tribes who watched the Lenape. Because we were the nearest to the coast, we were the first to make trade with the Europeans. In some cases that created envy, because by the time trade items got to the interior, they were the leftovers. Plus, with each exchange those items cost a little more as they went further into the interior.

There was one other very serious situation that came from that European contact, and it even continues today. Europeans traded for beaver pelts and the Lenape received a gun. Then, as they developed that trade and were getting guns and gunpowder, those tribes from the interior who did not have guns became alarmed. Here's a neighbor who has a gun and they don't. So it started an arms race that has come right up to present day, only today it's no longer just tribe against tribe. This arms race includes the whole world. It went from bow and arrows with stone tips, to muskets with lead shot, to a button that can blow up a continent.

So the Europeans created an imbalance, and that caused a lot of conflict. Because we were one of the first tribes to make contact with the Europeans, we were among the first to get their diseases, which decimated our tribes. Many tribes disappeared from the face of the Earth. Those epidemics, and then alcohol and warfare, weakened the Lenape. Our numbers had fallen off terribly—that's when the Iroquois started to take advantage of us. As the Europeans forced us away from our homelands, we had to move into areas occupied by other tribes such as the Iroquois and the Shawnee. We were under their protection, but also their dominance, which led to conflict with the Lenape people. Prior to European contact, we had no conflict with the Iroquois, but the history books kind of skim over that. Those history books don't reveal why conflicts occurred after European contact.

By being the Grandfather Tribe to so many other tribes, the Lenape were highly respected by just about all of the Eastern Woodland Indian people. If we did not relate to them through marriages and blood, they respected us because we were a very respectable tribe. *We were the people who held the peace amongst all the Algonquin and Eastern Woodland people.*

## Lacrosse

Lacrosse is the oldest organized sport in North America. It originated with the northern Indian tribes. It was a very important sport in many ways. It helped to train young men for speed and endurance. It was a fun game, but with many of the larger tribes it served another purpose. Sometimes the larger tribes would find themselves in conflict with another tribe, usually over hunting or fishing areas. Rather than have warfare, they would organize a lacrosse game. The winner of the game won the right to use that hunting or fishing area for a prescribed period of time. It was a very rough sport. They had no forms of protection like they do today. Normally, they would strip down to a loincloth and moccasins or sometimes even barefoot.

That lacrosse stick was not just to sling balls. Sometimes it was also used as a weapon. Players might get a broken hand or a broken finger, but rarely were there any fatalities. Depending on the size of the tribes, there may be well over 100 players on the field at one time. The field could be a mile long. Sometimes they played for days, from sunup to sundown. In some cases, they smoked the pipe after the game. But often, the team that lost just wanted to go back to their villages. In the end, Lacrosse prevented the tribes from going to war.

I consider them a very intelligent people who had organized a game used to avoid warfare. A Ho Ka!

## Training for Braves

We referred to our young men as braves. We strove to train them to be strong physically as well as mentally. They were never called warriors because we were a peaceful people. Though they were able to defend themselves if need be, war was not a threat. There were many activities that were performed for fun that toughened a young man's body. There were games such as running, stick ball, wrestling, archery, and swimming. Training included learning to identify all the animals and knowing their habits. It also included how to fish, track, trap, stalk, and hunt the animals. Training also included Indian lore. One thing that was very important was to always tell the truth. It was important to learn at an early age because it prepared them to become responsible. It made it possible for the whole tribe and others to believe what that person said was the truth. Truth was *sacred!*

## Cradleboard Learning

The Cradleboard was used to transport a baby from place to place. It also played a very important role in the baby's development. If the mother was going to work in the garden, she strapped the baby in the cradleboard and put it on her back. In the garden, she hung the cradleboard in a tree. As she began to plant or pick vegetables, the baby watched its mother working. The baby saw the land, the woods, the sky, the clouds, and any animals and birds in its vision. The baby experienced all the colors of the fields, the fresh smells coming from the garden, and felt the wind on its face. The baby heard the sounds coming from all the birds, animals, and insects around the garden. In this way, the baby made a deep connection to the Natural World through its physical senses. Soon enough, the baby's perceptions of the life around it would be increasingly fine-tuned as it developed.

That afternoon, when the mother decided to return to the village, she took the baby down, strapped it on, and walked to the village. Then she hung the baby up in a tree in the village area. Now, the baby had a chance to see all the relatives there in the village, hear the language spoken, and watch all the activities that were taking place. The baby saw all the family relations, the backdrop of the woods, and all the sounds coming from it. That evening, the mother took the baby down from the tree and hung it inside the wigwam up in the top. Now, the baby watched the grandparents, the mother and father, and any brothers and sisters working and interacting. It saw the fire and all the activities of the evening, including preparing the evening meal.

The scientific world has discovered that babies carried in that fashion tend to develop mentally much faster. They realized that a baby lying in a baby coach or a bassinet only sees one element—the element up above. The babies hanging in a cradleboard or carried on the mother's back see everything from the ground all the way up to the sky. They see all the people, activities, and everything that's in their focus. Those babies develop a lot faster because they see life just as it is; they see it in all dimensions. So again, it's not just a means of transporting the baby from one area to another, it's also a learning experience for those babies. I consider them a very intelligent people to come up with a method like that.

**Home Sweet Home**

Living quarters varied from tribe to tribe across North America. The Lenape people lived in dome-shaped wigwams, and generally there was just one family in a wigwam. It was framed out with saplings with the blunt ends driven into the ground. The saplings were bent into a dome shape, tied together, and covered with reeds from summer to fall. In the wintertime, they used elm tree bark to cover their wigwams to keep the elements out. The cooking fire was usually outside, especially in fair weather. Inside the wigwam, the fire was used primarily in the winter or during foul weather. At the top of the wigwam was a hole to release smoke from the cooking fire. Generally, there was not a lot of smoke because the harvested wood for the fire was dry, dead wood broken off of standing trees. In foul weather, the smoke hole could be closed when people were not cooking. Families used an animal skin to cover the entrance. In good weather, most of their activities took place outside and they slept inside at night.

The Iroquois had longhouses—long rectangular structures with arched roofs. As many as twenty families lived in one longhouse. They were pretty big structures, but each family had their own private area within that longhouse. So our domiciles were a little different as well as the number of people who lived in them.

The tipi comes from the Western Plains Indians. Tipis were designed for open terrain. Those tipis are cool in the summer; they roll the sides up from the bottom. The air circulates; it comes in at the bottom and goes out the top. In the wintertime, they have an inner wall of skin that traps the warm air. It's a form of insulation. I learned recently from another Indian that tipis can withstand extremely high winds. Because of its curved shape, the wind would rush around the tipi, but not blow it down. The design of the tipi was discovered by a child, from a falling leaf that had curled into a cone shape.

Some young people ask me questions like: "Do you still live in a tipi in the woods?" And I laugh, you know. I tell them, "No, I get up in the morning and touch the wall, and I have light, and I have air conditioning. I turn the faucet, and I have water."

I kind of make a joke out of it, but there are people who think that unless you are living in a wigwam in the forest, hunting and fishing and gathering, you aren't an Indian. Kids will ask me how I got to the school that day, and when I say in a pickup truck, it's confusing for some. Fortunately, teachers know how to straighten that out.

**Party Time**

The ceremonies of the Woodland and Lenape Indians were related because their environments were similar, and they were cousins as far as the New England states. Socializing was very important, and a major aspect of that was the feast. Hospitality with the Lenape people was remarkable to the Europeans. William Penn made a statement about the Lenape that: “In liberality they excel, and nothing is too good for their friend.” They didn’t have to know you, they were just a very hospitable people, and there was always a feast. With ceremonies, marriages, games, and food, it was just a festive time when they came together.

Prior to European contact, the Lenape came together more for social events. That was how a lot of those marriages took place and how the other tribes became cousins of the Lenni-Lenape. Our influence went along with those marriages from the shores of the Atlantic Ocean all the way to the Ohio country with the Shawnee people. We were a highly respected tribe.

## The Significance of the Number Four

I look for meanings and signs in the Creation, which I can see and understand. In Nature, the Creator has given many signs, and one of those signs is the number four. In many ways we see this: The Cycle of Life begins with infancy, progresses through childhood, adulthood, and old age. We have the four seasons: winter, spring, summer, and fall. There are the colors of the four races of man: white, black, yellow, and red. There are the four winds and four directions: north, south, east, and west—and the four elements: air, water, earth, and fire.

We need all of these together to make our lives complete. These are just some of the things in Nature that come in fours. The Creator gives these signs, and they're also messages. They all belong and are all in balance. Four also has a special meaning to me because four people have led me down my spiritual path: my Grandmother Anna, my Uncle Copper, my brother Jim Three Buck, and Frank Fools Crow, a medicine man of the Lakota Tribe.

## Nations Within a Nation

Indian tribes were sovereign prior to European contact because they had functioning governments.

The first treaty between the United States and the Indians took place with the Lenape Indians. They were a nation within their own right in this land. Sovereignty is recognized any time a government-to-government treaty is established, and sovereignty was automatically established based on those treaties. Treaties were not just used for creating reservations. Often, the treaties were struck for peaceful reasons. When European nations were fighting each other here, they would seek peaceful relations with the tribes to prevent them from becoming allies with their enemies. Treaties really weren't the beginning of sovereignty. Our sovereign status was not something that came about because of involvement with the European or United States governments.

*Indian people have always considered themselves sovereign, and they were.*

## The First Reservation

There was a reservation at Indian Mills in Burlington County, New Jersey. It was the first Indian reservation in the United States. I think it was established around 1758. It was called the Brotherton Reservation at Edgepillock. It didn't last very long. The Lenape people who tried to live there found that they could not sustain themselves with the constraints they were given. Eventually, the people started to move away from the area to places like Ohio, Indiana, Michigan, and Canada. Finally, they abandoned that reservation at Edgepillock. I had heard that some of those Indians left and moved way out in the remote New Jersey Pine Barrens to live.

Some years later, a delegation of those Brotherton Lenapes who moved out west and to Canada came back to New Jersey and claimed they sold the land but not the hunting and fishing rights. Supposedly, they had been paid off by the State for the land. I don't recall the amount, but it wasn't a lot of money. The story goes that the State of New Jersey paid off that delegation for their hunting and fishing rights. According to the State, that was supposed to sever all ties with the Lenape Indians and their land in New Jersey. That cleared the books as far as the State was concerned. Well, I never gave those Brotherton Lenapes permission to sell my rights. The State paid somebody who then left. I don't want to let the government off the hook. They have done some really underhanded things.

I don't want the State to forget about the New Jersey Lenape people who never left.

## Fact or Fiction?

I do a lot of reading. Some of it is written by Native American Indians, and some is not. Some of it I can buy into, and a lot of it I don't. I try to keep an open mind for what makes sense, and I expect that from my students. In 1994, Professor Harry Gershenowitz of Glassboro State College in New Jersey (renamed Rowan University) heard my talk at the tribe's powwow at Bridgeton High School. He was impressed with some of the things I said, and afterwards asked if I would talk to his class, and I agreed. It was an opportunity for me because I had never spoken at a university or college before.

Before I started, he stood up and said, "Dick, everything I have ever read about the Lenni-Lenape here in the state of New Jersey is that they never really lived here, they just passed through." I knew what he was talking about because I had read that myself.

I said, "First of all, I want you to keep an open mind. A colonial farmer is plowing his fields in preparation for planting corn in the spring. A group of Lenape Indians approaches him and asks if they could get water from his spring and stop to rest. They always traveled to a location that had water. The colonials usually built their cabins near springs where the tribes traditionally stopped to drink and rest. After granting them permission, he asked them where they were headed. They told him they were heading for the Delaware River. That night, in his log cabin, in front of the fireplace, he wrote in his journal: *Group of Lenape Indians passed through heading for the Delaware River."*

"Then, early that summer, while hoeing his cornfield, he saw a group that had left the Delaware River approaching him again to use his spring and rest. He asked them where they were heading. They told him they were heading for the Atlantic Ocean. Later, in front of his fireplace, he wrote about that in his journal: *Group of Lenape Indians passed through heading for the Atlantic Ocean*."

"Then, that fall when he was in the field harvesting his corn he saw a group of Lenape Indians approaching him. They asked him for permission to get a drink from his spring and stop to rest. Again, he asked them where they were heading. They replied that they were heading for the dense forest, and he put that in his journal. Later on, someone read that same journal and copied that information. Someone else may have a diary with very similar information. Later on, somebody realized there were fewer Lenape people passing through and decided to write a book about them. He took those journals and diaries and used that information for his book. Eventually, someone else wrote another book and used some of that same information."

Then I said, "Well, what the original colonial farmer saw that spring was some of the Lenape Indians who were leaving their winter villages in the dense forest. They were heading for the Delaware River in preparation for harvesting the large schools of shad, herring, white perch, salmon, and rockfish that came up the river to spawn."

"Then, early that summer, that same farmer saw Indians who were leaving their river camps and going to the seashore. They also harvested at the seashore."

"In the early fall, they traveled back into the dense forest to prepare for winter. There, they trapped and hunted fur-bearing animals and gathered nuts and berries."

The European concept of "home" was that you lived where you built your cabin, your barn, your outbuildings, and where you had your garden, livestock, and pastures. Everything was fenced in, and they called it "real estate." That was their concept, where the Lenape concept was so different.

*We believed that land was a gift from the Creator for all to share, just as the air, sunshine, and water.*

We did not stay in one spot forever. We followed the harvest though the seasons in several locations. In the spring, we traveled from the winter villages to the Delaware River and Bay area for the fish migration. Later on, in the summer, we walked to the seashore to harvest fish, crabs, clams, and oysters. In the winter, we came back to our winter villages and camps in the forest. In that way, we gave Nature a chance to rejuvenate itself. The Europeans' concept was that life must be stationary, but we moved around.

The idea of our homeland was based on two things. First, that we had enough people to occupy the area to make the claim that it's the domain of the Lenni-Lenape. The other was geographical features, which usually determined our boundaries, such as a river or a mountain, or in this case, the ocean. The Delaware Bay, the Atlantic Ocean, the Hudson, and the Delaware Rivers were the geographical circumstances that determined the areas of the Lenape tribes. It was a concept different from the Europeans.

So, from the observations of those first colonial farmers, the written word was put into a book. Then, that book became another book, and pretty soon it became a "historical fact." But it was not a fact, it was an opinion. It became "his-story," the point-of-view of the "historian." The Lenape have always occupied what is now the entire state of New Jersey.

When I go into the school systems, I tailor my program for each age group. As I present to the older students, part of what I try to do is correct a lot of these fallacies. Because they were written, they were considered factual, when in a lot of cases they were merely opinions. Besides the school systems, I also speak at different functions, social events, and churches. Another common fallacy I try to correct is that we "worshipped" Nature. That is not true; we *revered* Nature and *honored* the Earth.

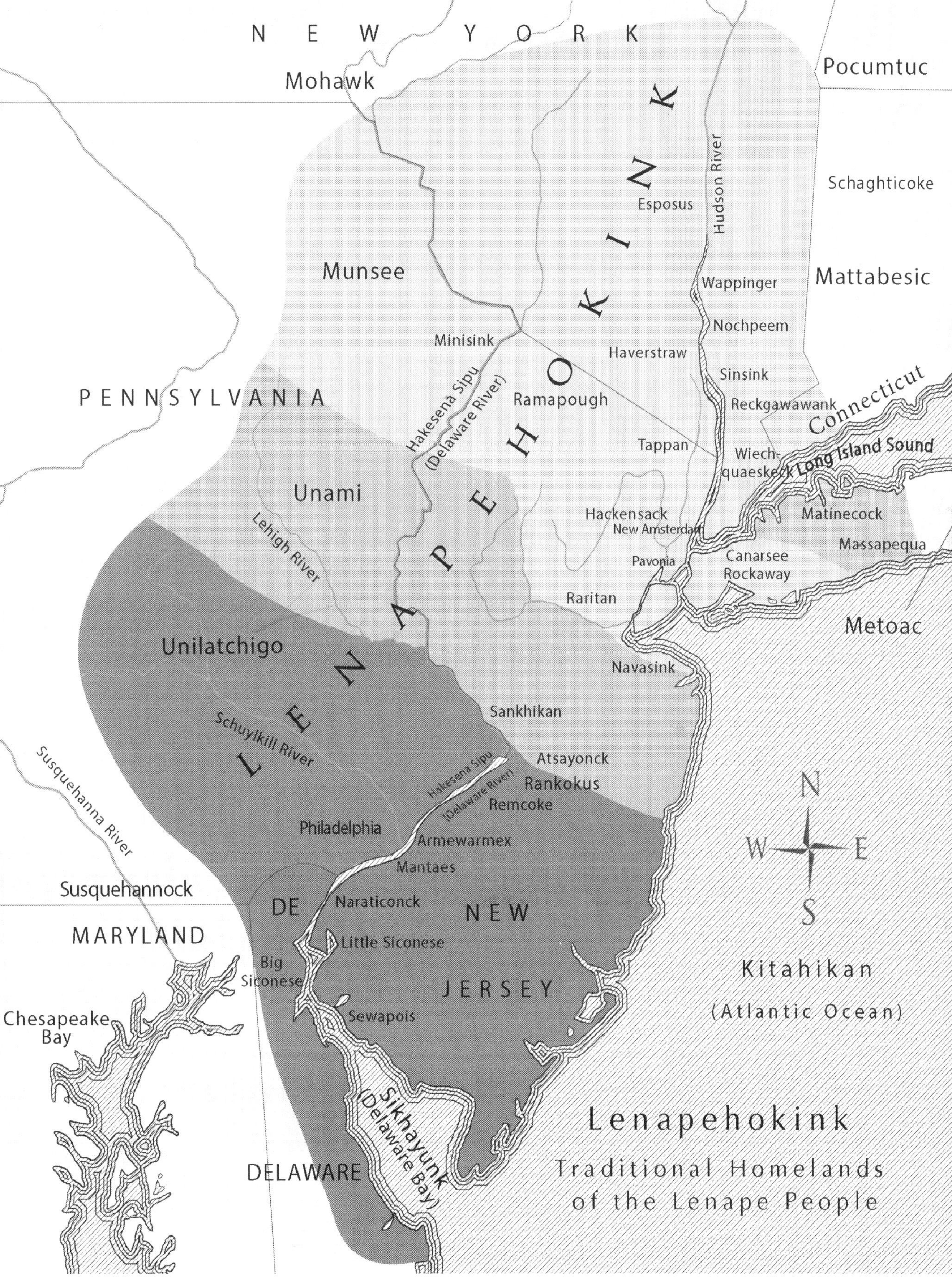
N E W Y O R K
Mohawk
Pocumtuc
L E N A P E H O K I N K
Schaghticoke
Esposus
Hudson River
Munsee
Wappinger
Mattabesic
Nochpeem
Minisink
Haverstraw
Sinsink
PENNSYLVANIA
Hakesena Sipu (Delaware River)
Ramapough
Reckgawawank
Connecticut
Tappan
Wiech-quaeskeck
Long Island Sound
Unami
Hackensack
New Amsterdam
Matinecock
Lehigh River
Massapequa
Pavonia
Canarsee
Rockaway
Raritan
Metoac
Unilatchigo
Navasink
Sankhikan
Schuylkill River
Atsayonck
Susquehanna River
Hakesena Sipu (Delaware River)
Rankokus
Remcoke
N
Philadelphia
Armewarmex
W
E
Mantaes
Susquehannock
Naraticonck
DE
NEW
S
MARYLAND
Little Siconese
Big Siconese
JERSEY
Kitahikan (Atlantic Ocean)
Chesapeake Bay
Sewapois
Sikhayunk (Delaware Bay)
Lenapehokink
DELAWARE
Traditional Homelands of the Lenape People

## Highways and Byways

Many of your highway systems today were once Indian trails.

Most trails were a little over three feet wide, just wide enough for one person to pass through the forest. Sections of some of those highways originally had been Eastern Woodland elk trails. The elk first made those trails and the Indian people traveled in back of them and they became Indian trails. The Lenape often walked through in single file when they traveled from one place to another. That's where the saying "Indian file" comes from.

If you look at many of the highway systems in New Jersey today, you will see how the Delaware River, Bay, and the Atlantic Ocean played significant roles in the formation of those highways and their directions. Route 9 skirts the coastline. Route 49 leads away from the Delaware River in Salem County and eventually winds up at the Jersey Shore. There are a few places on Route 49 (the Cohansey Trail) that you can investigate. Look for an area called Burden Hill; it is one of the high points in South Jersey. In the summer, after leaving their fishing camps on the Delaware River, the Lenape people began a journey to the shore. When they reached Burden Hill, they slept at a village there.

Their next destination was a place called Five Points, which is on Buckshutem Road on the east side of Bridgeton. Five trails came together there. About 500 yards further east on Buckshutem Road is another high point. My mother's people lived in that area. The Lenape travelers slept in that village. They followed those foot trails at a leisurely pace. They might stop along their way at a village and spend time with relatives or friends. There was no hurry. Then they would head for a place called Tuckahoe (on the other side of Millville). There were several villages there. Along the way, they may stop again to spend time with relatives at another village. They'd sleep at the Jersey Shore next. They would describe their trip as so many *sleeps* from one destination to the next.

They traveled to the shore for the large schools of fish, the crabbing, the oysters, and the clams. A lot of that harvest was smoked or dried and stored for the winter. Some of it was also put away for trade. So those were very important trails that eventually became today's highways.

As for the Eastern Woodland elk, the European settlers eventually hunted them to extinction.

## Old Indian Trails of South Jersey

## Very Special Indians

There are many Native Americans that I have a lot of respect and admiration for. One is the late Chief Roy Crazy Horse from the Powhatan Renape Nation. They are Lenape, only they pronounce it Renape. As I understand, that comes from the Swedish pronunciation. Roy's family is Powhatan, from Virginia, but most of the tribe was Lenape. He passed away a while back. Even though he and I had differences, I believe he had tremendous foresight. I spent a lot of time with him up on the Rankokus Indian Reservation in Burlington County, New Jersey. I learned a lot from him and I believe he learned a lot from me. In the mid 1980s, I was up there practically every weekend. Outside of his groundskeeper, Lone Eagle, and his council, I don't believe anyone else had a key to the reservation besides me.

*It gave me an opportunity to get back to what's important to me, which is my relationship with the land.*

One Friday morning I got there early and started setting up my display. The following week was the Columbus Day weekend when they were having a big shindig. They planned on having one every year on Columbus Day; this was going to be the first. I was setting up to do a cultural program. It was a village-type setting and the chief made everything available to me—anything I needed. I tried to gather as much material as I could from the forest and have it in its natural state. It was a misty, drizzly day. That afternoon at four o'clock the staff left that reservation like it was getting ready to blow up. The staff (with the exception of Roy and Lone Eagle) thought I was kind of strange for staying and setting up my village display in the rain. Roy told me and we laughed about it. Well, I was dressed for the weather and I really felt privileged to be there.

I was as happy as could be; I had 350 acres of the reservation with its forest, which was like my private playground. East of it was another 250 acres owned by the Audubon Society, and a game preserve. The western border was a farm where handicapped children stayed in the summer. The southern border was Rancocas Creek. I had all of that, and what I learned here about deer I never had an opportunity to learn before. Here, I could identify individual deer. I could watch that deer or look at the track and say well, that's such-and-such. I was stalking—not with hunting in mind, but just to be able to get close to a deer. It was all about being in the Natural World and being myself. That's what was missing and that's why Roy made it available to me. I must have seemed kind of strange to the staff, but Roy understood this was the Indian spirit that was missing. He used to say I was the spirit of the reservation because I loved being there and roaming around. He had a lot of foresight. He brought his tribe and all the New Jersey tribes a long way. He was a very intelligent man and well connected politically.

Frank Fools Crow was a Sioux medicine man. He once said he would not bring on a protégé. At that time, he had not found anyone who he felt he could pass down the knowledge and skills that he had. That's a powerful statement, but I can understand. He's been gone over ten years now; he was a very special man. I was in his presence at a Sun Dance in Maryland some years back. His insights were magical! The night before the Sun Dance we were down in this big glen around a bonfire. It was a time when each individual, if inclined, got up and said whatever was on his mind.

My brother Jim Three Buck and I were sitting next to Frank Fools Crow, and this man was talking to me with his mind. He didn't speak, but I could *feel* his communication.

*I had a strange feeling and broke my gaze into the fire and looked up at the treetops—there was an image of a buffalo in flight. In that vision there was also a circle of people around a fire.*

Some people might say, "It's your imagination" or "It's just a coincidence," but I know what I saw. My brother Jim saw the same vision. On the last day of the Sun Dance it was brutally hot and humid, and the water was just running out of us like a faucet. The Sun Dancers had been fasting all week and were exhausted to the point where they were staggering. It was a very clear day, but just before they danced, out of nowhere a cloud appeared, and then there was a sudden downpour. It lasted no more than a few minutes, but it was a drencher—then it was gone. It was just enough to cool down the dancers and everyone else. Everyone felt refreshed, especially the dancers who were suffering.

An Eagle appeared and circled that glen. Everyone was in awe of the sight. They said they hadn't seen an Eagle in that area in 50 years. Everything was right: the drumming, the fasting, the purification, and the prayers. There is no doubt in my mind the presence of the Creator was in that circle, and I attribute that to Frank Fools Crow—a fantastic man! He was the one who actually presided over the Sun Dance to make sure it was done in the proper way.

Chief Joseph was a 19th-century Nez Perce from the Wallowa Valley in Northeast Oregon. He had promised his father that as chief he would never sell the land where his father was to be buried. It was a classic situation. The settlers started pouring into their reservation. Before long, there were conflicts, and the settlers forced them out of their own reservation. The U.S. Army had soldiers from the Civil War who were sent west to pursue them. The Nez Perce fled all through Oregon, Washington, Idaho, Wyoming, and Montana. Chief Joseph had the responsibility for his whole tribe, including the elderly and the young. They got within 40 miles of Canada where they hoped to live. The people were so tired and worn out, and some of his chiefs told him they had to stop and rest. When they stopped, the Army soldiers came in from three directions and killed most of them. That was in the 1870s. Chief Joseph really was shown to be a good man just trying to protect his people.

Geronimo was portrayed as a cutthroat. Geronimo had 38 Apaches and the United States Army had 5,000 soldiers trying to capture him. Geronimo and his small band of Apaches eluded capture for over a year. He was portrayed as a bad guy because those 38 people had created that entire disruption to the Army and the expense to the government to defeat him. The Apaches, being the last, had not been conquered. That was one of the reasons they got so much attention. Geronimo was tracked to his stronghold by the Apache police and captured. It was really a time to exploit their success in capturing Geronimo—they could finally declare that the Indian wars were over.

Chief Seattle had a foresight that I find remarkable. He was a Coastal Suquamish Indian from Washington State. He died in 1866. It's a classic because what he predicted way back then is a reality today. Only someone with a keen insight into the future could have seen what he saw.

*He said, "What befalls the Earth befalls all the sons of the Earth. The fate that befell the Indian is what will befall the entire world."*

**Serving Their Country**

I'm sure you've seen the famous picture of the six Marines raising the flag on Mount Suribachi on the island of Iwo Jima during the Second World War. One of those Marines was Ira Hayes, a Native American (Pima). He is the Marine on the left.

In the First World War, it was the Choctaw: they were the first code talkers. You don't hear much about that, but the U.S. infantry used the Choctaw Indians and their language as a code.

In the Second World War, in the Pacific, it was the Navajo code talkers. They had a system based on symbols that only a traditional Navajo Indian could understand. For instance, they used the Navajo symbol for an Eagle, which meant a plane. A potato was a hand grenade and other things were symbolized from their culture. No single Navajo knew the whole system. There were more than 400 Navajo in the Marines trained as code talkers.

One Marine general said he feared we might have lost the Pacific war if it hadn't been for the code talkers. It's the only code that has never been broken, even today. Some believe their officers were instructed to kill the code talkers before the Japanese got a hold of them if it looked like they were going to be captured. They saved a lot of lives. On July 26, 2001, more than 50 years after the end of the war, President George W. Bush awarded the Congressional Medal of Honor to those code talkers. As an interesting side note, 79 years before those code talkers served in the war, their grandfathers' families had been forced by the U.S. Army to march to a desolate reservation in the Southwest. Many Navajos were killed during what was called The Long Walk. More than 25,000 Native Americans served in World War II, and by Presidential Proclamation, November has been designated as National American Indian Heritage Month.

I had a unique experience on July 4, 1998. One of the original Navaho code talkers came to speak at a local VFW in Dover, Delaware. He talked about his part as a code talker. It was very interesting. During the course of that program, Charlie Little Owl Clark made a presentation. (Little Owl is the son of Kenny Red Deer Clark, who was the chief of the Nanticokes at that time, from the lower Delaware, Millsboro area.) Little Owl was up on the stage and he had a young male Nanticoke dancer with him. After the code talker finished speaking, different Legionnaires came up and presented him with a plaque or a framed commendation. Then they introduced the son of the chief.

Little Owl said, "Well I don't have any framed pieces of paper to give you, but I have some traditional Nanticoke herbal medicines and an honoring dance for you." The dancer was in full regalia, which was very colorful comprising of a ribbon shirt, a breechcloth, and feathers. It was a very energetic dance in a circle on the stage, and the feathers and ribbons fluttered with each movement. The deer toe rattles he wore on his legs kept the beat of his dancing. When the dancer finished, I could see that the veteran code talker was very moved by it. I was elated to see the way Little Owl presented the traditional Indian gift and expression of thanks. I had never met Little Owl before but I had heard about him and had seen him in different circumstances. I thought that was very cool. That demonstrated real meaning and significance to the Navajo code talker compared to some pieces of paper with words on them. Since then, Little Owl and I have become very good friends.

When we met he said, “I have been hearing about you.” I guess I was new to the state and a lot of people said they heard about me.

I had started getting a lot of news coverage and they said, “There for a while I thought you were the only Indian in the state.” I wanted them to know that whatever it is that I have, it is coming from the Natural World. It’s my way and connection to the Natural World.

My father and Uncle Copper were in the First World War. I don’t know if they served together because they didn’t talk about it. Uncle Copper was really a closed-lipped person. That wasn’t unusual back then. A lot of the older men didn’t talk a lot. I don’t know if it was because of the persecution they experienced, or just a common way that they were. Maybe it was both. The only time I saw him open up was when he was drinking—then he would *really* talk.

Copper’s outfit was one of the first that got hit with mustard gas. His outfit got devastated. What saved Copper was a dead mule. He cut its belly open and crawled inside and stayed for several days. When he came out the mustard gas had dissipated. But his outfit got messed up bad because they weren’t ready for it. My brother Jim said Copper used to get a government check because of that mustard gas episode but I don’t think it was much.

## The Lenape Way of Life

The Lenape way of life was based on the land and the environment. The environment had a lot to do with the things they thought and talked about. Winter was a story-telling time, because they spent a lot of time inside their wigwams. Oral history was vital because we didn’t have a written language. Once, a person asked me a question about how our people lived because of what he had read about Indians. He had gotten the impression the people weren’t really all that bright, that they were kind of backwards. He wasn’t being smart, it was just the way he had envisioned it. I thought: Well, how am I going to handle this?

I said, "Our people were *very different* from the Europeans and their way of life. Just to show you how so fundamentally different they were, women could walk bare-breasted and it brought on no sexual connotations where the man was concerned. Women's breasts were not designed for the man; they were designed for the baby."

I think that comment kind of made him do some more serious thinking. I couldn't go into a big detailed explanation about the differences between the Europeans and the Indians. Our thinking and way of life was just so different from the Europeans.

I believe one of the things that triggered the Europeans' dim view of us was because we didn't have a written language. They figured that if we didn't have a written language we couldn't be too bright. The written word has carried, and still does carry, a lot of weight. But in many cases, I can take that written word and easily show that things were actually not the way they were written.

It was a culture that really worked. Everything seemed to be perfect for the way we lived and the way we looked at life in general. It was a very simple way, but a very effective and sustainable way. So today, there is an entirely different view of the Indian, a more educated view. Life before was a lot simpler.

Oh, for the good old days when the sky was the roof, the ground was the floor, and life was so simple. It must have been a beautiful way to live! A Ho Ka!

# 3.
# THE NATURAL WORLD

*"Man does not weave this web of life. He is merely a strand of it. Whatever he does to the web, he does to himself." -Chief Seattle, Suquamish*

## Learning Patience

During the winter, my father went to an area of Deptford Township, New Jersey to cut firewood. It was a big oak forest with a lot of nut trees. That's how he made his living in the wintertime. He and my Uncle Copper also made wooden hoe and axe handles. I remember watching them sitting in the back yard making those handles. For the last scraping, they used glass to get that smoothness before they applied linseed oil. They seemed so relaxed sitting in the backyard making those handles. Their patience always intrigued me.

As I got older, I had the opportunity to spend more time with my brothers Ralph and Jim. Out of all the things they taught me about Woodbury Creek—the hunting, the trapping, and the fishing—the most important was *patience*. You had to have patience. Knowing the *rhythm of the creek* was important, because there were certain times when the fish and the animals were a lot more active than usual.

They taught me how to totally occupy myself with my surroundings. The first time it was Ralph and me on that bank on Woodbury Creek; it was one of our favorite fishing spots. He said, "Listen…tell me what you hear."

I started listening—the red-wing blackbirds' calls were very prominent. I remember telling him how striking their sounds were to me. I told him I could hear them way across the creek in the meadows.

He instructed me to listen to all of the bird sounds, so I started listening to the sounds of all the other birds. Instead of being impatient, I found myself listening and watching. That occupied the time where normally a young person gets anxious or fidgety and wants to move on to other things. *Ralph and Jim showed me how to take the time to observe and listen.* Once I got that digested, sitting still was natural for me. After learning patience, every time I went to the creek, I'd listen for the red-wing blackbirds and all the other sounds in that area.

Back then, wild rice was plentiful and a big food source for the red-wing blackbirds. As the tide changed, I could hear the intensity and volume of the sounds going up, down, or sometimes totally quiet. It was like somebody turning up the volume on the radio real loud to a crescendo and then bringing it back down. After that, I could distinguish the faint sounds of the insects in the meadows. I guess you could call that a sound rhythm. It was a pulsation of all the sounds together. That was the first time I realized that there was a sound rhythm, not just in the meadows along the creek, but in the woods too. It was the rhythm of the creek that followed the tide.

*This was like a doorway that I stepped through into the Natural World.* It was something I looked forward to. This is how Lenape children were taught to connect with this world.

Another sound that I heard was the carp splashing, jumping out of the water, and bucking the tide. It also felt cooler as the tide rose, and warmer as it lowered. When I was out there alone, being in the woods and along the creek in particular, I was just a young kid absorbing the Natural World. Everything outside of Nature was someplace else. The birds, in particular, were active in the surrounding woods. I used to get a real kick just sitting and observing the rhythms of the creek as the tide rose and fell. At certain cycles of the tide the birds got very loud. They had to be communicating with each other. At other times they were very quiet, but they were still contacting each other. They were telling each other to get ready—the insects are out, or whatever it was they were feeding on. I loved it. *So, I learned the rhythms of the creek and patience mostly from Ralph and Jim, who have a deep understanding of Nature.*

## How I Caught an Ancient Fish

When I was about nine years old something exciting happened along Woodbury Creek. It was an experience of a lifetime, one that I often like to replay in my mind. It was early June, on one of those beautiful spring mornings where everything was alive and the air was cool and clean. We had a thunderstorm the night before. I remember waking up during the night and hearing the thunder and seeing lightning. I went out to the creek early, just about sunup, to fish. I was in an area of the creek that no one went to besides my family. It's way through the woods at the back part of the creek. There was a sandy bank with excellent fishing where two parts of the creek came together. We would fish each tide. At certain levels of the tide, the fish will bite when the small fish they feed on are active. At other levels, they stop biting when these small fish become inactive.

I had been fishing for about an hour and caught some catfish. The tide had gotten low, and the fish stopped biting. I was sitting on the bank, feeling the warmth of the morning sun, listening to the red-wing blackbirds, the insects in the meadows, and the sounds in the woods. I was waiting for the tide to get low enough so I could go into the creek and start spearfishing. One part of the creek went off into the meadow and the other part was the main branch. There was a mud flat right in the middle. I watched the tide go out until it was about waist deep. I was getting ready to wade in to see if I could spear some fish when I saw something moving out from the far bank—it was a huge fish!

I had never seen a fish this big. I was thinking that this was an exceptionally large carp. So I started easing into the water towards that fish to get close enough to spear it. I was getting really excited and my heart was pounding. Well, the fish started to get a little edgy. I slowed down, moving closer. All that existed now in my world was that fish, the spear, the creek, and me. I could tell the fish was getting ready to make a fast getaway, but I wasn't very close, so I threw the spear as hard as I could and hit him in the side. That must have confused him, because instead of swimming away from me, he swam towards me to deeper water. As he passed, I reached out and grabbed the end of the spear. I was a skinny little kid and this huge fish pulled me right off my feet and dragged me down the creek. He was so powerful, he dragged me fifteen or twenty yards, but I was able to force him up onto that mud flat.

It was exhilarating! This fish was huge, and he was thrashing and I was trying to hold him down with my spear. My heart was pounding fast, so I took some time to calm down and relax. The fish was about five feet long, which is a monster compared to the fish I had seen. But it wasn't a carp. It was very strange looking, not like anything I'd ever seen—I was very excited! It felt like something very special had just taken place that might not ever happen again. I was fortunate that the spear hit the fish in the side and not in the back. Its sides were soft, while the back was like armor plate. I made the spear with a jagged center prong, so it hooked the fish when it went in. That's why the spear didn't come out as he dragged me down the creek. Now I had to manipulate the jagged part to get it out of the meat.

The tide was still going out and I was struggling because he was still alive and flapping, but he was getting tired. Now I was able to drag him into the water, off the mud flat, and

onto the bank. It took me quite a while to drag that fish up the hill to Evergreen Avenue, and it took me a long time to drag him home that afternoon because I had to stop often. My father said that it was an Atlantic Sturgeon. He said that when he was a boy he watched sturgeons come into the creek to spawn. Now I know what they look like, but I had never seen one in the creek before, and I never saw another after that. I heard they were once plentiful in the creeks, but something changed and they stopped coming up into the creek. I think it must have been hilarious to see that big sturgeon dragging a skinny little kid down the creek.

That was one of the highlights of my many episodes along Woodbury Creek, one that I will always remember. I have the same type of fishing spear that I show the audience when I do programs. I tell them about that episode with the sturgeon and how that type of spear is one of my favorites because of that experience. I love telling about it.

### A Hunter's Best Friend

Sport was a very unusual dog. Let me tell you how he came to us. Jimmy Clark was a friend of our family, and before I was old enough to hunt with a gun, he went down to visit relatives in Virginia and brought back a pup. He didn't look like a hound dog; he had small ears and light-brown colors. Down there they let the dogs roam free, and we could tell he was a mixed breed. When he'd scare out a rabbit in high grass, he jumped up trying to see where it went. A hunting dog that didn't run or use his nose was of no value, so Jimmy didn't think the dog was going to be any good. I was around 12 years old, and that summer I was out in the woods every day, so I'd take Sport with me. He soon settled down and started to use his nose. I told my brother Harry that I thought he was going to turn out to be a good hunting dog. Harry offered to buy the dog from Jimmy, who I think sold him to

Harry for $12. Jimmy went around telling everybody what a fool Harry was for buying a dog that was no darn good. Then, we came to find out that Sport was the best dog that has ever been around.

This dog was special. I remember one occasion when there was a wood pile in my neighbor's yard. I noticed Sport was digging down under that wood pile, which wasn't unusual; he was always digging and doing something. I realized that he dug down there and came out and circled over to one spot. Then he went back and dug under it again. So I got curious and walked over to see. What he had done was dug down under that pile and killed a mother rat. The rat just laid there. I watched him dig down and go under and into a nest. He was bringing out these little pink baby rats one at a time on his tongue and laying them out in a pile. He did not kill them, but he killed the mother. I didn't know what to make of it, maybe compassion? Anything that was wild—he was on it. He caught more rabbits than the average hunter could shoot.

He wasn't a big dog. But he was the only dog I know of, especially that small, that could take on a coon and win. People heard about this dog and came from miles around to see him. Anyway, when Jimmy Clark found out what a heck of a dog Sport was, he offered to buy the dog back for $300. Back then that was a ton of money. Harry wasn't interested in selling Sport. Sport had become part of the family. Once I was old enough to hunt, Sport and I were out in the woods all the time. If I was hunting with my brothers and Sport got on a rabbit, nine out of ten times either one of us would shoot the rabbit, or the rabbit would go underground and Sport would dig him out. Sometimes the rabbit went up in the hollow of a tree and I'd take a length of bull briar vine, twist it up inside, get it caught in his fur, and pull him out. Or, sometimes I'd smoke him out. If he stayed on the ground, Sport would catch him. He was like greased lightning. The dog was a fantastic hunter.

He supplied us with a lot of rabbits, even after the hunting season. We didn't have to bring a gun; he'd run a rabbit down and bring it back. There were times after the season when I took Sport out in the woods in the snow, built a fire, and fell asleep. Now, I'm not shooting the juice to you, but when I woke up there were two or three rabbits lying next me that Sport had caught—and he didn't eat them. And he was smart. If a rabbit ever did get away from us, Sport remembered that rabbit. Any time we went back in that area, he stopped, turned around, and looked at us like: Do you remember that rabbit that got away from us here? Well, he hunted up that rabbit until either we shot him or Sport caught him.

I'll tell you about one time where there was a big briar patch and he knew there was a rabbit in there. The dog had a fantastic nose. He charged right in that briar like he was right on the rabbit and then cut around to the other side and caught that rabbit coming out. I thought that was pretty amusing. We figured he was mixed with hound dog and bird dog. He wasn't a big dog: average size, slender build, small ears. But he didn't look anything like a typical hound or bird dog. You know, a lot of people just couldn't believe the stories and had to come and see for themselves.

He was so fast that one time Harry was shooting at a rabbit and a pellet hit Sport in the eye. It blinded him in one eye. Now, I know you're going to say this is a lie, but he was a better dog with one eye than he was with both of them. A lot of people wanted to hunt with us because there was always going to be plenty of rabbits. Many of those guys couldn't hunt or shoot, and we always made sure they got a rabbit. So, quite naturally, they liked to hunt with us. I didn't particularly like it, but my older brothers let them hunt with us. In Deptford Township, there was a big meadow out near the piggeries. There was high ground, and then a drop off in a big, low, open area. People had used the sides of that high ground for dumping. See, if a rabbit went in a hole or off under something like a dump pile, Sport would go in there and get him. He'd dig to China if he knew a rabbit was in there. Anyway, the rabbit had gone under one of those dump piles, and Sport went in there and chased him out.

I was down in the bottom in the saw grass, while everyone else was at the top. When the rabbit came out, it came running right towards me. One guy, Johnny, threw up his gun to shoot. Fortunately, I saw it, because if I hadn't I'd be blind today. I turned my back when he shot at the rabbit, and that shot splattered along that saw grass and all up my back. In those days the hunting coats were made out of canvas. Fortunately, I guess because it was canvas, and maybe the distance, that hot lead had stung me, but it didn't penetrate. My brothers made sure that if they shot, there was nobody in line of sight. But some of them other guys were greedy hunters. They'd shoot you and think nothing of it.

I remember Jim and I were down at the creek one time, and a rabbit ran inside a muskrat tunnel and under the bank. Sport went digging in there after him and dug himself out of sight. The tide started coming in, and oh man, we called and tried to get him to come out. He was way up in that hole and wasn't coming out. The tide finally came in and covered the banks and we thought for sure he was done. Then, about 20 yards in from the bank, we saw the earth shaking. Sport came digging up through the ground—and he had the rabbit!

Another time, we were hunting in Swedesboro, New Jersey, near Swedesboro Lake. It was the first time we'd ever hunted there. Sport had been running a rabbit and come late that afternoon he hadn't shown up with the rabbit. It was getting late and it was time to get out of there. We started calling and calling for Sport, but no Sport. It got dark, so we decided we would come back early the next morning on Sunday and see if we could find him. Now, Swedesboro is about 11 miles from Woodbury. Well, on Sunday morning we woke up and guess who was on the front step? Sport. Now you explain to me how he did it; there is no explanation that we could come up with. We never hunted there before. We don't know how he got back to Woodbury, but he did. The dog was incredible.

### Ghost Rabbits

We called them Ghost Rabbits. You could not kill them. They are the big ones, at least half a size larger than a regular rabbit, and they know a lot of tricks. Part of their survival mechanism is that their habits are different. They travel differently. I think they are a special breed. Because they are individuals, you don't get a fix on them like you do when you find a lot of rabbits or deer in the same area. Sometimes you had the bead on them, but you never hit them; they were meant to survive.

It's been a long time since I was in that situation, but this winter (February 2013), I find it happening more. But then, I'm being told it's because I can't shoot anymore. Maybe I'm calling them ghost rabbits because I can't shoot. But I *can* shoot—and I laid the shot yesterday. I missed him the first time, but on that second shot I rolled him. So I can still shoot. They are always on the run. On the going away shot they don't stand a chance, but on those side shots I find I'm not leading him enough, I'm shooting in back of him. When I was meat hunting, I took them anywhere I could get them. I dug them out or smoked them out of their dens. I hunted them anytime I needed to. That was right up into the 1940s. That's not the case now; I might give them a running chance. These ghost rabbits will not feed where other rabbits are feeding during the day. They don't stay around the rest of the rabbits; they kind of isolate themselves. I think it's because if there are a lot of rabbits in an area; it draws attention.

I'll give you a for instance. I was 14 when I had my first encounter with the ghost rabbits. It was the first year I was eligible to hunt. Back then, in the area where I grew up, there was a lot of game, but towards the end of the hunting season, the rabbits got scarce. I would seek them out in spots like old abandoned piggeries where there were a lot of honeysuckle vines. The other hunters neglected those spots, but I always hunted those areas, and I found rabbits that nobody else did. One of their survival mechanisms is to stay out of sight. There are a lot of reasons for this, just like a buck deer.

I'll give you an example of a wise old buck. To avoid being seen, he'll feed at times when other deer avoid the feed, like at night, or on cloudy, rainy, or overcast days. So he was not exposed as much as a younger deer. He finds an area where he can hide out, and if someone does come seeking him, he usually has himself in a setting where he can see, smell, or hear that person in advance. In other words, the hunter has to come to him. That's how he gets to be an older deer with the big racks. Some of these deer are larger than the rest. I guess it also has a lot to do with their genes. The same thing applies to bigmouth bass. They stake out their area, and it's usually an area with brush or lily pads, someplace where they can hide. They will lay in ambush and wait for the baitfish to swim by. They will stay in that general area, because it gives them protection. Now, say if that deer is killed, or that bass is caught, another deer or bass will soon occupy that same area because the area fits their natural instinct and keeps the balance in those areas.

That also applies to the ghost rabbits. They usually come around at night to feed. Sometimes they'll feed during the day if the weather is going to get bad, especially with a big snow when food is difficult to find. They will feed to get filled-up before the snows come. When the snow does come, their eating habits and choices will change, because what they normally eat is covered with snow. That's when I start to see where they've gnawed the bark off of trees, bushes, and twigs, because they can't get down to the grasses or vines of the honeysuckle. Sometimes I can tell how big the rabbit is by how high up the bark is chewed off. We had a lot of honeysuckle and wooded areas. Some rabbits preferred the woods; other rabbits would rather be in a field or hedgerow. The weather and the sun plays a big role in where they go. When it gets cold, especially the night before, they like to sit out on the edges of the briar patches and hedgerows where they can get the morning sun. When the cold, windy weather begins, especially if there's snow, they will usually leave those open areas and go into the woods to find brush piles or thick areas where the wind can't get to them.

A while back, I was coming up from the creek and was walking along the edge of an open field. It was late afternoon, and I had not found any game. Well, I had a pretty sharp eye at that time, and I detected a slight trail leading out of the hedgerow into that open field. In the middle of this field was one tuft of Indian grass. I walked out to it and found a ghost rabbit. He had dug down under this tuft of Indian grass, and he was huge. That's how he had survived. No one thought to hunt that open field. He had been hiding out in that field, I guess, most of the season. I had him and he knew it. He knew there was no way he was getting across that open field without me getting him. Our eyes met, I saw his eyes get wide with fear. I had him dead to rights—and I let him go. It was the first time I had ever experienced that kind of fear from an animal I was hunting and the first time I let one go. It wasn't that I felt sorry for him. I felt that with all the cunning he had used to escape, it just didn't seem fair to take his life. It was an emotional experience for me, and that wasn't the case growing up. But then, I think that was the first time I looked at a wild animal in the sense that he was entitled to make it through the season. Because he was large, and a survivor, I knew he was a breeder. All his survival skills would be transferred to his offspring to ensure the future of the rabbits in that area.

I still go rabbit hunting, and it's always exciting to me. It's a chance to get out and do a lot of walking, and for an old-timer like me, I need all the walking I can get. But the kill isn't that important anymore. Once in a while, I will get a really big rabbit, but most of the exceptionally big rabbits don't show up until the middle of January. That's when I start finding those big ghost rabbits. They are usually the smart rabbits—they survived. Some days we might get one rabbit and some days not get any. For me now, it's really just about being out there tramping around in the woods and enjoying Nature. I really enjoy listening to the dogs run and being out there in the Natural World.

## Migration of the Eels

When I was around 11 years old, I watched the amazing migration of the eels. There's a spillway at Clark's Pond near Gouldtown, New Jersey. Water flows over the spillway into a wide area of fresh water. From there it flows into the Cohansey River. Small eels were coming up from the Cohansey into that wide area of fresh water—thousands of them! They were working their way up the spillway and through the root systems along the stream bank to get up into the lake. They were making it, too. I didn't understand what was taking place at the time, but it was a fascinating sight. Once they got up the bank, there was an area about two cars wide where they had to cross the land, and then they were in the lake. I always felt kind of privileged to be able to see a natural occurrence like that.

## The Shad Roe Industry

There was a big white sandy beach in Brooklawn, New Jersey, right on the Delaware River. The shad migrated up the Delaware along that beach. People used horses to pull nets and drag the shad up onto the beach. The shad that had roe were thrown in a pile. They didn't eat the shad with the roe; they didn't think the roe was good to eat. My father used to get that shad roe and my grandmother cold packed it.

Cold packing is a system of preserving the roe in jars. We fried the roe; it was a big breakfast food for us. Doctor Pedrick from down in Pedricktown got wind of my father taking the shad roe. I don't know how he found out, but he found out my grandmother was cold-packing that shad roe. He made an industry out of it.

I remember my father talking about that beautiful sandy white beach. It was right on the mouth of Big Timber Creek on the Delaware River. I have a large poster describing that area the way it is today and all the different animals and plant life you can find there. It really explains just how much life is in that one area, all kinds of trees and animals—you name it. You will see all kinds of life, but the deer there are very elusive; you don't see them often.

**Hold Your Breath**

Here is something interesting: a good cure for a bee sting—mud. There's even a way to avoid bee stings. You will probably laugh, but—hold your breath. At an early age I learned to hold my breath if any yellow jackets, bees, or wasps were around me, or any time I felt an insect on me. That gave me a chance to get that insect off. I watched my father lift a wasp on his finger, and it was trying to sting him. I saw the stinger trying to go in his skin but couldn't. He explained to me that your skin is covered with pores and when you hold your breath, your pores close up. Whenever you feel an insect, or you anticipate an insect on your body like a bee or wasp, quickly hold your breath. You can see him hitting with his back end trying to inject the stinger, but it won't go through. You might get little surface welts, but with the pores closed, the bee can't get the stinger through. My dad read some of Dr. Goodbreed's books on anatomy and other books on medicine. I think that's where he might have picked up that information.

This does not work for mosquito bites. Mosquitoes are a different ballgame, because of their proboscis; it is so thin that it gets through your skin, but a bee's stinger can't. Now, if you do get stung, apply mud. That tends to cool it, calm it, and draws the poison out.

## A Secret

My Uncle Copper had a tree that grew many different fruits. One year it had apples, the next year pears, the third year it had peaches, and the fourth year it might have some of each. I watched him sitting in the backyard sharpening his pocket knife. Sometimes he sharpened that knife for an hour. When he made his cuts and grafted those limbs together, they were perfect. And when he inserted them in the slot, I couldn't tell they had been put together.

He had a secret. It had something to do with the sap. He cut out a groove and put sap in there. Then he joined and tied the limbs together. There was something about the sap, I think, that had a lot to do with keeping that life flowing, which caused his success with his grafting. Somehow, word got out about that tree. I believe it was Rutgers University that sent a couple of professors to try to get Uncle Copper to tell them how he did it. It was either during or right after the Depression years. He never divulged the information.

When I got older, I gained a new perspective on what else was going on. Looking back, I realized that during those hours he sat in silence sharpening his blade, he was praying. He was asking for the power to make sure that what he was doing was going to be right. He had a real gift when it came to plants. Many of the houses in East Woodbury and the Delaware Street area of West Woodbury had landscaping that my Uncle Copper designed. That's where the wealthy people lived.

## The Hunter and the Hunted

When I was about 14, there was an incident where I felt like an outlaw. In the area I hunted and trapped, there were three large gullies with streams that came down through the woods and merged into one stream. Way in the back, about a mile from Woodbury, that stream went down into Woodbury Creek. Well, the southern side of Woodbury Creek was a borderline for acres and acres of land belonging to a man named G.G. Green. He was a colonel in the Civil War. He was a very wealthy man; at one time he owned all of East Woodbury. The game warden let plenty of game loose on Colonel Green's property, so there were always a lot of game animals. I believe he was dead when I was coming along,

but his descendants were still there. They had a big mansion. I used to really get a thrill crossing over the borderline into that land.

One day I was on G.G. Green's side, and I shot a pheasant. The caretaker had a red pickup truck, and I heard him coming from the mansion because the tailgate squeaked. By the time he got there I was back on the other side of the borderline or hiding somewhere. He would cuss me, but he never came into the woods. Then, I heard the tailgate squeaking as he drove back. I went to another area of the property and shot something else. Then, I heard him again.

I could imagine how the Plains Indians felt when they raided the horses of another tribe or Robin Hood poaching the king's deer. I knew I was breaking *his* law but I didn't feel as though I was breaking any laws where I was concerned. It was thrilling, even though I realized there could be severe consequences, which only heightened my interest. I did that periodically, just for the thrill of it.

## The Keen Eyes of the Hunter

Stalking came naturally to me because I spent so much time outdoors. I considered myself very good at getting close to animals without them knowing I was there. Patience was the key. My father taught me to *walk little and look a lot.* But being able to blend into an area and then ambush deer didn't take place until later in life when I went to the Pine Barrens to deer hunt. In the area where I grew up, there were no deer around. Now they are everywhere. But back when I was growing up, we had to drive a considerable distance to the Pine Barrens to find deer. Europeans put so much pressure on the natural environment that the deer were killed off in populated areas. The Pine Barrens was the only place they could survive because it was an isolated wilderness.

*When I first started bow hunting in the Pine Barrens, I hunted the old way—on foot, with my bow.* I took 12 steps and stopped; then, for about 20 minutes, just looked. What this entailed was taking in the terrain, the direction of the wind, checking the ground for moisture on the pine needles, noticing animal trails and tracks, as well as signs of deer such as scat, chewed leaves and stems, rubs, and scrapes. I listened to the rhythms of the forest. Then I took another 12 steps, stopped, and looked.

In this situation, as you get closer to your deer, the intensity starts to build, and your heart beats faster. When you know that he's just beyond the blueberry bush in front of you, you try to raise the bow in a slow, deliberate manner without shaking, which would alert the deer. The shot is always directed to the heart. The key is to make your shot when the deer is in a relaxed state and totally unaware of your presence, so you can drop him quickly. A deer that is alert is like a coiled spring. He can bolt as soon as he hears the snap of the bow string. He can't react quickly if he is relaxed or very close. That's why stalking is so important—the element of surprise.

Deer tracking is very interesting. If I have the time, I locate a herd in an area with a lot of deer. Then, I observe closely so I can recognize each individual. Once I get that down, I start to recognize individual tracks. Let's say I spot a mature buck. I can distinguish him from the other bucks by the shape and size of his antlers. Once I recognize that deer and see him walk along a fire lane or trail, I use a tracking stick. It is five or six feet long. I find a clear track print, and then lay the tracking stick down so the end of the stick begins at the front of his track. I take a rubber band and wrap it on the stick to line up with the heel of that

track. That indicates the length of his toes. Then, with that same stick, I measure the front of the front toe to the heel of the back toe. This is to measure the deer's stride when he is in a relaxed state. Now, I can lay that tracking stick down on the tracks and tell if that was the same deer because of those measurements marked with rubber bands. So, now I've got that individual down when he's calm. Then, when I see that same deer in an excited state where he is walking rapidly, I measure those tracks.

That way I get the complete read-out on that individual deer to where I can look at that track and tell it's the mature buck. I can do the same thing with the doe. I can make individual tracking sticks for each deer, so I can look at the tracks and tell which deer it is. Now, some say no to this, but I have seen it work.

But when the deer is running and leaping, I have to go to visual tracking. Some say you can't distinguish a buck track from a doe track. You can, but it takes a very keen eye, and a very clear track, and all the other things I described.

Have you ever seen a buck deer? During mid-autumn, a mature buck's neck expands because he has all this fat stored in his neck and a lot of energy. During the rut (mating), he is very active and has to depend on this stored fat because he doesn't have time to eat; he is strictly involved in the rut. If you look at his front tracks, you will see how they sink deeper in the ground because of the extra weight of his antlers, his head, and thicker neck.

There is another way too. His back track indicates that it's a buck, because the weight is more on the inside of his track. Now, this takes a very keen eye. With the doe, by being a female, her weight is on the outside of the track because of her pelvic structure and carrying the baby. These are things that take a lot of practice. You have to know where the deer are at certain times so you can get those visual readings and then use the tracking stick.

The Lenape, like other Indian people, were very aware of the animal life in their area. The hunters watched and learned from the coyote. The coyote is known as the trickster—a very intelligent animal. My people learned how to herd and ambush deer from watching the trickster. Their survival depended on knowledge like that. They learned from the successful predators, and the coyote is one of the real smart ones. Along with the deer and the coyote, they paid particular attention to the bear. In the fall, the bears are fattening up and getting ready for hibernation. They watched the sow make her den and where the boar made his den. Now, if they found themselves in a situation where they needed to harvest a bear, they wouldn't go into the den where the sow had wintered because she has her young during the winter. They went into the boar's den.

That was a dangerous time. They used different methods to hunt the bear. One was to smoke the bear out; then the hunters would shoot it with arrows, or use spears. If it wasn't possible to smoke the bear out of the den, they had to crawl in with a spear. Sometimes the hunter caught the bear asleep or in a kind of semi-awake state and could kill it. But other times, the bear woke up and killed the hunter. It was very dangerous! I like the idea that they would not harm the mother bear and her cubs.

The Lenape learned about the Natural World at a very early age, because that was like the university to them. It was the Natural World they lived in, not today's man-made world. So being a people who depended on the Living Environment for everything, it was second nature for them to observe the bears to make sure they did not disturb the female and her young.

After I retired from my job at Mobile Oil, I moved my family to Delaware where my wife's people are from. It's really too warm to bow hunt as early as September when the season starts here in Delaware. For instance, if you get a deer in the afternoon and it's not a shot where you killed it outright, you have to track that animal. In early September, the woods still have a lot of foliage, and tracking can be very difficult because when the deer bolts, he quickly disappears behind the foliage. If you don't get that animal before nightfall, it has to lay in the woods overnight when the coyotes can get it, and because it is warm, it will spoil. So, I don't like to bow hunt here because the season comes in too early—it's still too warm. Besides, it can get downright uncomfortable moving around in the heat. Bow hunting in New Jersey is different. It comes in October where there may be warm days, but nights are cool. If I don't find my deer by nightfall, I might have to leave the animal in the woods overnight. The next morning, I'll pick up the blood trail, and because it was cool that night, the meat will still be good.

## The Birds

*Everything in Nature has a definite pattern and purpose.*

Watch the mockingbirds. They sing all night, and during the daytime they are protecting their areas. They are territorial and guard their food sources. The berries on the holly and dogwood trees are their main diet. They eat insects too, but if there are mockingbirds around, I can bet that those two trees are somewhere close by. We always had the mockingbirds around our house when the berries were ripe. My father sometimes clapped his hands and listened to them trying to duplicate that sound. They never got it quite right, but I could tell they were trying to imitate that clapping sound.

Until recently, I hunted quail and pheasant. I have hunted woodcock and dove in the past, but I don't hunt them anymore. Woodcocks are getting scarce. Mourning doves are very good eating. Back when I was growing up in New Jersey, there were very few doves, nothing like it is today. It was a rare occasion to see a dove. There was a gravel pit not far from our house, and there were pine and white birch groves on high ground around the pit.

I remember hearing a dove cooing. I was intrigued by the sound. I had never seen or heard one before. I was curious and crept in, and then I saw the dove up in a pine tree. I didn't know what it was. When I described it to my brother Ralph, he told me it was a dove. Over the years, I have become very fond of them, especially around the house. I don't have the heart to hunt them now.

Another interesting bird is the blue jay. I see the blue jay as an Indian. I relate to him because he's very secretive. There were many blue jays around where I grew up. They were there, but I wouldn't know it. I guess that's an Indian spirit I like. They love to raid, and they communicate with each other. Sometimes it's voice-wise, and sometimes visually. When they do it by voice, it's usually when they have scoped out the area and there are no people around. They are signaling the boys, you know: "C'mon, there are lots of acorns here," or some corn, or whatever it is they are marauding.

They also have another way of communicating. It's with a flash of their blue and white feathers. When they move their body a certain way, that white flashes. It's like a mirror-type thing and it must travel for long distances, because I'll look and only see this one blue jay. He will do that flashing and not make a sound, but after a while, I'll see others appear. If you ever hear loud screaming from a group of blue jays, they are probably chasing off a hawk or an owl, or even yelling at a cat near their nest.

The crows are also raiders. Around late spring, they'll be raiding the grackles' nests. These crows are crafty. One or two crows will quietly sneak in the neighborhood in the early morning and hide. They already know where the grackles have their nests. Then, one crow will fly in making a lot of noise, which alerts all the grackles that there's a raider in the area. If you listen, you will hear a crow making that gurgling sound, and you can tell they're setting something up. The grackles will all come out of the trees and chase the crow off while he's squawking at them. The crows that were hiding quickly sneak in and steal the babies. While the grackles are chasing the decoy, the other crows rob the nest. They're very crafty.

*When I was growing up, being around Nature was what stirred my curiosity.* It was a time and a place where I could do that, and I didn't have the problems or the pressures from society like there are today, so these things came naturally to me.

### A Balancing Act

The digestive system of many migratory birds is designed for the areas they migrate back and forth to. It's a balancing act.

The food that's abundant in one season at one location may be different from the food in another area they will migrate to later. During the summer season, their digestive system allows them to take in insects. Then, in the late fall and through the winter, their digestive system changes to digest seeds. The basis for that is this: during the warm months when there are lots of insects, there will be plenty of birds. The baby birds hatch at the same time the insects hatch, so there is plenty of food for the parent birds to feed their young. These birds keep the insects in balance. Seeds from different plants become abundant in late fall and winter, so their system changes to digest seeds, such as with the sunflower and the bull thistle. Some birds like berries. They are part of Nature's means of creating abundance. They digest the fruit and spread the seeds to different areas, increasing the population of those berry plants, which provides more food for the birds.

You see how Nature has allowed for these things?

### A Chain Reaction

As a boy coming along in New Jersey, I never saw geese in our creek.

In the late fall, I watched them flying high to wherever they were heading. Delaware and Maryland were places you could find a lot of geese in the wintertime. A chain reaction took place when farmers started to plant cover crops like winter wheat, rye, and clover that held the soil in the wintertime. So the geese didn't have to go as far south as they used to. They started to stay further and further north because they have a food supply now, and the winters aren't as cold and long as they were, due to the changing climate. Well, gradually, over a period of time, they stopped going to the end of their range much further south. This is migratory disruption. Man has now upset a migratory system that has been in place since ancient times. Now, instead of those geese going south, they stay north. To most, that wouldn't represent a problem.

The Creator set this migratory system in motion a long, long time ago. Those birds had been following that system longer than anyone knows. Now, because of man's agricultural system and the warming climate, that has been reversed. What those birds may have fed on in those southern states, they no longer go there to feed on—so that sets off another reaction.

The animals that may have fed on those birds now have to change what they feed on because those birds are no longer available.

## The Creator's Design

*The Creator designs everything in this system. That's why it all functions precisely.*

Now to some, these migratory changes are no big deal, just Nature readapting. Some species can adapt and some can't. But the main thing is that man is disrupting a natural system that has been put here by the Creator. We don't know what those changes will create. They could very well create a catastrophe.

I had a discussion with an educated man about this *balance of Nature*. My point was that there are certain species in some areas that no longer have their natural migratory system. They will die off because they won't be able to adapt. The food sources won't be there and they are not designed to adapt to other foods. They will die off.

His words were, "Survival of the fittest."

I said, "Yes, but when they die off, that's a part of a natural balance that no longer exists."

He said, "Well, that's no big deal, Dick, because the dinosaurs disappeared."

I said, "True, the dinosaurs did disappear, but that was not because of man. That was the Creator's design. And when the Creator takes something out, the Creator puts something back in its place to maintain a balance. It's that the Creator understands, not us."

When we destroy a species, we do not put anything back that fits in its place. His suggestion was that the dinosaurs disappeared and nothing happened. Well, the Creator did that—not man. When man destroys a species we have no idea what will happen. We don't know how to inject something in its place to maintain that balance. Usually, when we replace something that has been destroyed, the replacement is worse. We are just starting to realize that Nature is getting out of balance—*big time*. To me, Nature is what makes everything work. If we get away from that understanding, and we get caught up in materialism, our priorities start to change.

*With these new priorities, our thinking gets out of balance*—then we cause this upset in Nature.

I am not a scientist, and I don't profess to understand the scientific world. I try to look at these things from the simple perspective of a traditional Indian.

## The Invasion of the Chipmunks

I'll tell you a little thing about chipmunks from personal experience. There were not many chipmunks where we lived when I was growing up, but on occasion we'd see them in Deptford Township near Woodbury. It was a pretty big township, but there was never an abundance of chipmunks. In the late 1940s and early 1950s, after the Second World War, many people moved into Deptford Township from places like Camden, New Jersey and Philadelphia, Pennsylvania. That was when the housing boom started.

When I was growing up, most of the roads in Deptford Township were unpaved. They started to blacktop the roads because of the population explosion. At night, the black snakes came out to lie on the asphalt to absorb the heat it gained from the sun. Well, so many people have this fear of snakes that they kill them every opportunity they get. Many people ran over the snakes—some accidentally, and many deliberately. As they killed off the black snake population, all of a sudden they had a huge population of chipmunks. It was epidemic! People couldn't figure out why the chipmunks were suddenly appearing in such numbers and destroying their landscaping. The chipmunks moved in around those houses and developments and ate the flowers and shrubs. Their normal food source was acorns,

but when they spilled into Deptford, there were few oaks left so they had to eat what was available. Some people were really getting into trouble because they started shooting at those chipmunks. So the law had to come in because they were shooting in restricted areas close to homes.

To this day I doubt they realized that the black snake was the main predator of the chipmunk. That's what kept the natural balance. When they killed off those black snakes, that balance became upset and the chipmunks overpopulated. Whenever that upset happens, a backlash comes about. So, that's just one of the things I have observed over the years. Chipmunks are really cool. They have beautiful colors and are so amusing. I can sit and watch them for hours.

## The Plight of the Mussels

*When I was growing up, there were freshwater mussels in great abundance in the rivers and streams around Woodbury.*

I spent most of my days on the banks along Woodbury Creek. There were clusters of those mussels everywhere on the rocks and roots along the creek. When I got hungry, I waded in at low tide and gathered those freshwater mussels. I ate them with a plant called wild pepper. Those mussels were a very tasty food. There were thousands of them everywhere. I remember telling my father about them.

*There were fundamental changes taking place in our environment, rather subtly—but things were changing.*

One summer, there just didn't seem to be as many mussels as there used to be. I told my father they weren't as plentiful, but he didn't comment on it. I wasn't alarmed because I had been taught that in Nature, there are cycles. There is a high cycle and then a low cycle. I just thought this was one of those low cycles. A couple of days later, I went down to the creek when the tide had gone low and the fish stopped biting. I was waiting for the creek to get low enough so I could catch the fish under the rocks with my hands or with a spear. There were very high woods, which led to the creek bank, and two trails. One was up along the top of the ridge and one down along the creek. My father came down the trail along the creek bank. It was a beautiful spring morning. We just sat there listening to the red-wing blackbirds and insects in the meadows.

When the tide got low enough for us to wade in, there was something he saw that I had missed. *In the mud on that flat where I caught the sturgeon, there were little pools of light, filmy oil.* My father noticed it.

He said, "I believe that's what's causing the mussels to disappear." Somehow he knew it was not normal for those mussels to disappear like that. He figured there had to be some reason for it. Well, it was during the beginning of the Second World War, and the industries along the Delaware River involved in the war effort were dumping into the river. Now, at that time the word pollution was never used. If it was, we didn't know about it, but my father knew something was causing that oil. We found out later it was from the war effort where they were dumping into the river. That pollution got into the back creeks. Mussels are a bivalve, and they get their sustenance directly from the water. They filter the water

through their system to extract their food. They are one of the first to be affected by it. I had always been taught and understood that Nature was all-powerful and all-controlling.

*Then, to find out later that man had the kind of power to cause a species to disappear—that really frightened me.* I thought Nature was all-powerful!

I haven't seen a freshwater mussel in those creeks since the Second World War. By the end of the war I could still find some freshwater mussels on a few of the older farms. They were in the streams and the woods way in the back parts where the water was still clean. Those areas wouldn't have been affected by the pollution as much as the regular creeks that flow into the Delaware River.

*In the tidewaters, those mussels had disappeared.*

### They're All Gone Now

Because we were on the East Coast, we were in the Atlantic Migratory Flyway. Every year, we could see thousands of birds migrating between the North and the South. My Uncle Copper told me about the millions of passenger pigeons in the 19th century, and how, in their migratory flight, the sun was blocked out for hours. The passenger pigeons are all gone now: killed—extinct. The Lenape were aware of whole forests being annihilated and completely destroyed. The Pine Barrens in New Jersey was originally a mixed hardwood forest that reached all the way from the Delaware River to the Atlantic Ocean. It was primarily chestnut trees, oaks, hickories, and walnut trees with some pines mixed in. Giant cedars grew in the swamps and along the streams. All were cut down: first the hardwoods and cedars for the colonies and for export to Europe, then the pine trees to make charcoal. Charcoal-fired furnaces produced cannonballs, cast iron, and glass.

Atlantic white cedars were huge. They were cut down and used to make cedar shingles and siding for buildings in colonial towns like Philadelphia. They were also used in the shipbuilding industry.

**Nature Gets Even**

*As a boy spending so much time in the woods, I never remembered a mosquito or tick problem.*

If I went into an area of the deep swamp, I might have run into a swarm of mosquitos, but overall, mosquitoes were never any problem in the creeks, the fields, or woods. As for ticks, once in a while I found a tick on me, but nothing like it is today. The tick problem now seems to be everywhere, even in your backyard. This is an indication to me that Nature is out of balance. It goes much deeper than that; I believe Nature fights back. I will give you a for instance: we have diseases now, such as Lyme and West Nile disease, that we didn't have when I was growing up.

*There were no insect-borne diseases that I can remember.*

If you go into Nature now, these are just a couple of the new diseases man is susceptible to. I believe this is one of the ways Nature fights back, because when modern man goes into the Natural World, he generally disturbs it. Even if he just passes through, there is a certain amount of disruption that takes place. Usually, it's more than just passing through. He either leaves trash, or he destroys something that is a part of that natural system. Well, I believe these diseases from different insects are one of the ways that Nature keeps man out of those areas. I have mentioned this in programs, and afterwards people will say things like: West Nile isn't even from here, it came from someplace else.

*I believe Nature works in unison throughout the universe.*

Even if West Nile came from Africa into this part of the world—all things are connected. I believe that, in Nature, the universe is a continuing energy—a circle: no beginning, no end. The West Nile virus is a disease that was designed for checks and balances in Africa, not here. But these diseases can travel with the bird migrations, and a disease in Africa can travel here. That is the universal connection. Once it came here, it spread quickly. That is an imbalance not just subject to this area; I believe it's a part of the entire universe. I don't argue these things. I am not a scientist, nor do I want to get into a situation where I am challenged on the basis of scientific studies. This is my belief, take it or leave it. I am not going to beat up on you if you don't believe me, but I don't want you to beat up on me if I don't believe you.

## The Ice Age

I sometimes hear the weatherman saying the weather we are having is average. I don't know when they started keeping track of the weather patterns, but none in over the last 50 winters has been average to me. I base it on this fact: we used to ice-fish every winter, not for a day—but weeks! We ice-fished in a place called Collins Cove, on the Mullica River in southern New Jersey. The water there is brackish and has a current. Brackish water is salty, and takes longer to freeze than fresh water. If that ice wasn't at least six inches thick, we didn't go out on it. If you went under, you weren't coming up, because you would never find the hole you broke through. I remember we went there and camped on a Friday afternoon and stayed the whole weekend ice-fishing. When we came back, we had grass bags full of white perch, and everybody in the community got some fish.

*I don't believe we've had many winters in the last 50 years where you could actually ice-fish.* If you could, it would only be for a day or two. When we ice-fished, it was sometimes for three weeks straight.

Someone once asked me if I could predict the weather. I wish I could. There was a time when I could, and it hasn't been that far back. There were certain things in Nature that indicated the weather, but not today, because Nature is out of balance. Here's a for instance: say a cloud formation comes over the Chicago area, and it draws things up from the Earth

such as steam, mercury particles, aluminum, or whatever is in the air. Water vapor is also drawn into the clouds. The prevailing winds may take those clouds across the Great Lakes. Then, when they get on the Canadian side, they dump those pollutants that came from the industrial areas. Those pollutants go into the lakes, rivers, and waterways and poison the water and its inhabitants. The clouds dump prematurely because they are loaded with more than just vapors drawn from the water in the Illinois area; now they are loaded with all those pollutants. This creates acid rain, which poisons lakes and forests. So, if those clouds had only been dealing with natural moisture, they would have dumped in a different location. That is probably one of the simplest ways of looking at it. In the past, there were certain signs in Nature. My grandmother could watch the ants and tell if there was a heavy rain coming. Well, I don't know if you can do that today. The ant populations have been affected by this upset in Nature just like everything else—just like *we* are upset. We are out of balance too, even though we don't think so. I hope I am getting the point across why I can't predict the weather now.

What brought on this conversation was when I did a program outdoors in the backyard of a pre-school called Tomorrow's World. It is all oak trees. I have been doing my program there for five or six years now, and the oaks are usually loaded with acorns. The ground was just covered with them. This time, I noticed there were hardly any acorns. I made a comment about it, and the teacher said she had not paid that much attention. When she

asked me if I could predict the weather, I told her there was a time I could.

I have oak trees in my own yard, and I usually have a pretty good crop of acorns. The blue jays came around hunting for acorns in the early fall, which was an indication that things were right. He's an interesting and very clever bird who will gather acorns. If I was in the yard, he wouldn't make any sound. If I am not in the yard and he comes, he sounds off and lets all the rest of the blue jays from his family group know that there's an acorn crop. One year they began scouting much earlier than usual, and the acorn crop was nowhere near what it normally was. That very well could be because in Nature there are cycles. It could also be because of the drought we had a few years before. The trees are still suffering from that drought. So there are many situations in Nature that prevent me from getting a clear view of what will take place. People used to be able to look at the squirrels and tell by how many acorns they buried or some animals by how thick their fur got.

I'll tell you a little story. When I was 14 years old, I was visiting a good friend, Woody Conquest, an elder who lived out in the country. It was a nice autumn day, and I was hunting in the swamp in back of his property. I always liked to go there, because there was a spring at the edge of the swamp right where his property started. I used to stop there and get a nice, cool drink. He had an outbuilding in his backyard. One day, he brought out a bottle of homemade peach brandy. We were sitting in the back yard enjoying the sun and drinking this brandy, and a woolly caterpillar came by.

I was going to show him how smart I was, so I said, "Mr. Woody, you see that caterpillar?"

He said, "Yes, I see it Dick."

I said, "You see how it is black on both ends and brown in the middle?"

He said, "Yes."

I said, "That means that the beginning of the winter is going to be severe, then it's going to be mild, and it's going to be severe on the tail end."

*He said, "Dick, all winters are severe; there is not one that is not severe."* Well, what he was saying was the wintertime is always tough, regardless. So, that's my little tale of the woolly caterpillar.

I can't predict the weather anymore. Sometimes it changes so abruptly that I can't keep up with it. I don't know about your meteorologists; sometimes they have been right on the ball, other times they are totally off, and they make a scientific study of this. Once, on a clear sunny day, my grandmother told me we were going to get a heavy rain in the afternoon. She was right. This may seem strange to you, but my grandparents, parents, and my Uncle Copper would make a statement like that and not tell me why. I had to watch and listen and try to figure it out for myself. Now, if it was important and I couldn't figure it out, then it was permissible to ask. But they spoke in parables, which I had to unravel. Sometimes I could, and sometimes I couldn't.

I've had people ask, "Why didn't they just come right out and tell you?" Well, use your own brain. It forces you to think. If they give you all the answers, then you are not learning to think independently for yourself. I believe that's what going to schools and college are for: to teach you how to think. Sometimes I wish I'd had a chance to go to college.

## The Living Desert

When I was in the Air Force in Yuma, Arizona, I knew an Italian civilian whose name was Giuseppe. Originally an immigrant, and in his fifties, he worked at the base during the week. He was also a prospector and had a mine up in the mountains. He and I got friendly, and every Saturday we went out to explore the Yuma Desert. Giuseppe really helped me to get familiarized with that desert. He was one of the most knowledgeable people I've ever met when it came to the weather, minerals, geography, and animals in that desert. He was the only non-Indian I ever met, besides Tom Brown Jr. (The Tracker), who could speak Apache. Apache is a difficult language to learn. Giuseppe taught me quite a bit, and two things especially that probably saved my life.

First, he told me about not looking under things. We had just started up into the foothills. I was down on my knees trying to look under a ledge when he put his hand on my shoulder and pulled me back. He always carried a single-barrel, 12 gauge shotgun. He took that gun and jerked the barrel under that ledge and out rolled a big rattlesnake.

He said, "Dick, during the heat of the day, something lives under everything. If it's no more than a grain of sand, there's an insect that hides under there, ducking the sun."

That was quite an experience. Well, that saved me from making that mistake in the future. Nothing moved around too much during the day, unless it was disturbed and pushed out. I might see a roadrunner, but once that sun came up and it got hot, everything tried to find a cool spot. The big lesson was telling me about flash floods.

He said, “If you hear rumbling off in the distance like thunder, get up on high ground as fast as you can.”

One time, I was down in a dry gulch when I heard a rumbling way off in the distance, just like thunder. I remembered what he told me about the flash floods. So, I got up out of that gully on high ground, and within minutes I heard it coming. It sounded like a freight train—whoosh—here it comes with water, cactus, coyotes, lizards, and snakes rushing right past me. I was only six feet above it. It came down that dry gulch, and as fast as it came, it was gone. That one would have killed me!

There were also peccaries in that desert (like a small wild boar). They feed on a certain kind of cactus. I saw their tracks, and on occasion I heard them in the cactuses feeding. But they were back in there where I couldn’t see them. I had read about them and I talked to different people who knew things about the peccary. They were quite a curiosity to me. I had never seen one other than in books and illustrations. To be close enough to hear them but not be able to see them stirred my curiosity. But those peccaries are slick. Whenever I'd come upon them, they got away from me before I could see them. Now, in the cactus where they hide out, those thorns look like ice picks. If I barged right in I was going to get "cactused-up." These peccaries are not real big, but they say they can be vicious. I've never had a problem with them. One time I did see them. From a high spot, I quietly laid down on a ledge and I watched them feeding below in the cactus.

There was another type of cactus, which the Mexicans called the jumping cactus. If you got too close to it, chunks of cactus would come off on you. If they got on you, you had a problem. When those barbs stuck in you, anywhere you took them out you're going to rip some flesh.

I wanted to see everything that was in that desert. One animal I wanted to see but never did was the Gila monster. I saw his tracks, and I saw where he had robbed a quail's nest of the eggs, but I never saw him. He would go underground during the day to avoid the sun. Gila monsters are venomous; the venom sacs are in their gums. They chew on their prey and that extracts the poison from their gums into the wound.

When they portrayed the roadrunner in the cartoons, they truly had studied that bird; they had him down pat. When I saw them running, they were so fast all I could see were little puffs of dust where their feet hit the ground. Once, I saw two of them gang up on a rattlesnake. The rattlesnake was trying to get from one section of the cactus to another to bed down, I guess because the sun had moved. They caught him out in the middle. Oh, they're clever too. One distracted him, you know, got in front of him and flapped his wings; the other one came up in back and pecked his head, or he'd fly up and just stomp his head. Once they got the head messed up, it was all over. Nature is something! When you see the animals out there doing their thing to survive, it's quite an education. Every time I went into that desert, there was something new that caught my eye. I pretty much saw everything that was in that desert except for the Gila monster: I saw the roadrunner, I saw the coyote, the fox, the rattlesnakes, the owls, the quail, the rabbits, the tortoise, and various lizards. I experienced the flash flood, and Giuseppe even took me up in the Superstition Mountains to see the Lost Dutchman's Gold Mine. That was quite an interesting sight.

People say the desert is dead. Not *that* desert—that desert was very much alive!

**Doctor Dolittle and the Lawyer**

Below Ferguson's Farm, down in Maryland, there is a swamp with tall trees and a small cove. We had ceremonies on the property and would camp right there on the banks of the Potomac River. Well, one Friday evening in late September, we camped there, and that night we had a big bonfire, with dancing and drumming. My oldest brother Harry and I were sleeping in the back of my old pickup truck. There was a tent next to us, and sleeping in that tent was the Piscataway peoples' lawyer and his son. His son was about nine or ten years old. That night it got kind of cool, and in the morning when I got up it was still chilly, so I started stoking the fire to warm up. Eventually, the lawyer came out. He was a non-Indian guy. We sat there and talked. A little later, his son came out.

Over in that swamp, in those tall trees, the crows started talking to each other. So I stopped talking and I started listening; it was pretty intense as the crows were planning their day. Have you ever heard how the crows talk to each other? Well, the lawyer, right away he thought: Oh, this is going to be fun, you know—he thinks he's Dr. Dolittle.

He said, "What are they talking about?"

I listened for a while. I said, "They are planning where they're going to send their scouts out." I saw a big grin come over the lawyer's face.

He said, "Well, what are they going to do?" And the little kid, he's all ears.

I said, "They are going to send their first scout up to Ferguson's Farm." So the little kid, he's getting excited. I listened a little more.

The lawyer said, "What about the next one?"

I said, "They are going to send him across the river. A little bit later, they are going to send the next one over to that tall tree by the cornfield that was hit by lightning. Then, a little later, they will send the next one over to the tree that leans out over the cove." So, the lawyer's got a big grin on his face, but the little kid, he's really excited. About ten minutes go by and out comes the first crow straight to Ferguson's Farm. Well, the little kid—he doesn't know what to think, but the lawyer's got this look, like: Yeah, right, you got lucky on the first one. A couple minutes later, the next one comes out and flies across the Potomac River. So now he's thinking: Well, two in a row—maybe he just got lucky again. A few minutes go by, and the next one flies out to the tree that got hit by lightning by the cornfield. Now, that logical mind of this lawyer, he's thinking: Let me see, well, maybe he's just very

lucky. The fourth one flies out of that swamp right to that tree hanging out over the cove. Now the little kid is *really* beside himself: This guy understands bird talk!

Over the years I've run into that lawyer at different Piscataway functions and every time, the first thing he says is, "How did you do that?" He thinks it was some kind of magic trick.

I said, "Well, I've observed how the birds communicate. I know they are talking about the local food sources." But he has never accepted that. What's that thing with Sherlock Holmes? "Elementary, my dear Watson!" This is from years and years of watching the crows. The crow is an interesting and very intelligent bird.

In the early morning, the crows are planning their breakfast. The first one that flew out went up to Ferguson's Farm. There are always some goodies up around the farm for a crow. There are manure piles and scraps, and they normally will send the first scout to the East where the sun comes up. Most birds and animals are attracted to the warmth and energy of the sun in the morning.

That first night when we got to Ferguson's farm, people were finishing up a picnic out on that big lawn at Mount Vernon, across the Potomac River. Everybody knows that crows realize there are always some goodies left over from a picnic, so that's where the second one went.

The third one went to the tree that had been hit by lightning, because that's where the cornfield was, and everybody knows they love corn.

That fourth one, when he came out of the swamp, went to that tree that had been undermined and was hanging out over the cove. When the Potomac River flows to that outcropping, it causes a swirling effect into that cove. That means it is always going to wash some dead fish or something to eat up on that beach.

Now, those scouts fly out to investigate, and then they send the message back. They are calling and telling the others that there are some goodies over here, or the corn is ripe, or whatever it might be. But that lawyer, to this day, still thinks it was a magic trick of some kind. His mind will not let him think that it was *not* magic—that it was some kind of trick. So that was my experience with the good lawyer and his son.

Over the years, I have been watching the birds. That's a part of what I've learned from spending time alone in the forest. The crow was always a bird that fascinated me as a boy growing up. I knew they had this communication thing amongst themselves, and it was always a bird that I spent as much time observing as I could. I am only skimming the surface here. Prior to European contact, the Indian people were much deeper into this than I am. They didn't have anything to distract them from that learning. They made it a point to learn all about the animals and Nature.

*We received our understandings and lessons from Nature and all of Creation.*

## You Are Not So Big

After taking basic training in the Air Force, I was stationed for three months at Geiger Air Base in Washington State. My first experience with a waterfall was in a place outside of Spokane, Washington, called Moses Lake. I used to go out there and spend weekends with an Indian family I knew. There was a creek that ran in front of their cabin. That creek was not real deep. In its deepest area, it might have been up to my neck and crystal clear. I was always curious about water; I wanted to see where water began and where it ended up.

One Saturday morning, I was up early. I started walking and following the creek. I had been walking for several hours when I started to hear a faint rumbling off in the distance. I kept following the creek as it got narrower. As that rumbling got louder, I could feel dampness in the air. It was in a section where the cedar trees came almost right down to the stream. As I stepped around the cedar forest, I saw this beautiful waterfall. I'd say it was about 100 feet high, and maybe 50 yards wide—a fascinating sight. I remember just standing there, amazed. I had never experienced anything like that and it made a lasting impression on me.

I often reach back to that scene because it gives me the strength to say to myself: Well, you think you are hot stuff, but next to Nature's grandness, you're not so big; *you're just a grain of sand in the overall scheme of things.*

# 4.
# CULTURE AND TRADITIONS: PAST AND PRESENT

*"With my arrows, I have the yellow, the red, and the green, which indicates it's a Lenape arrow. For my personal markings, the colors are black, yellow, red, and white. These indicate the four races side by side, as I believe the Creator has meant for us to live." -Chief Quiet Thunder*

### Traditional Village Life

When I describe the Lenape people, I'm mostly talking about my tribal ancestors from southern New Jersey.

As I understand it, we didn't have large villages like the Lakota Sioux. I think 12 wigwams were considered the average size. Those small villages were scattered around, but were connected to each other with footpaths. Villages were built near water and food sources in the forest where they wouldn't get the full blast of winter. The distance between villages varied from a mile to 30 miles to ensure they were not competing for their resources. Many villages were located in forests where game was available year round. The elderly and the children who could not travel stayed in their villages, while other members of the tribe traveled to their seasonal camps.

Village life was fun, exciting, and very rewarding. Each day brought a new adventure. There was so much to do and learn, but it was at your own pace; nothing was urgent. Individuals started their day every morning by first washing themselves at the stream. Then, each person stood and faced east, and prayed as the sun rose. There were many ceremonies where they came together, but that Morning Prayer was done individually. The people enjoyed many activities in their villages, and each season had a special excitement and ceremonies—especially spring.

Spring was the time to seek out the wild strawberry patches. All through early spring we periodically checked to see if the strawberries were ready for picking. When they were ripe, that was a big time! Harvesting strawberries was a family event. It was fun for the little ones because while gathering the strawberries, they probably ate as many as they put in their baskets. Those wild strawberries are as sweet as sugar. Strawberries are the first spring fruits and contain a lot of power and medicine. After a winter without fresh fruit, we always looked forward to the strawberries. The Lenape people considered those first spring fruits a very special gift from the Creator, so we performed ceremonies giving thanks.

After the strawberry harvest, other important events took place, such as planting the garden, the corn, and spring fishing. It was exciting when large schools of fish came up into the creeks and streams to spawn. All the young boys and girls were taught how to catch those fish. One of the methods we used was the stone fish trap. The older boys, who were 11 to 14, gathered large rocks about the size of footballs. They waded in the stream at low tide, and stacked those rocks in a V-shape formation about a foot high. They left a very small opening on one end just big enough for a fish to get through. Sometimes they made very large V-shaped traps, and sometimes rather small ones, depending on the size of the creek and how many people were involved.

Once they got the stone trap in place, they played a game with the little girls and boys ages four to eight. They instructed them to take a small turtle shell, or a basket, and gather pebbles, stones, acorns, and seedpods. Once they got those containers full, the older boys took the little ones into the stream at low tide. They lined them up across the stream facing the open side of the V-shaped stone trap. They instructed the little ones to walk slowly towards the trap and toss those pebbles, acorns, and seedpods in front of them, making a splash. The water was just below their knees and they were splashing and having a good time. Splashing excites fish. When fish become excited, they tend to come together and school up. As they swam away from that line of little ones tossing pebbles, they entered the V-shaped trap. Down the other end where that small opening was, the older boys were lined up and waiting with spears. They speared those fish one at a time as they passed through the small opening.

Now, this was a very important learning experience: they were having fun, but they were learning at the same time. That was the very beginning of tribalism for them—they

were learning how to cooperate as one group. Tribalism begins at that early age. After the fish were speared, the older boys handed them over to the girls who were ages 11 to 14. It was the girls' job to butcher the fish. Cleaning fish was not easy. Sometimes they used a knife made from a deer's leg bone, and sometimes it was made from flint, or even obsidian. They then opened up the fish and took the insides out. They used a deer's jawbone to scale the fish. Then they cut the meat into thin strips.

The older boys built a very hot fire, usually with oak, and let it burn down to coals. They placed a drying rack over those coals. A drying rack consists of four corner posts with green saplings lashed across them. They spread thin slices of fish across the saplings. The heat from the hot coals dries and cures the meat. It also keeps the insects away. Sometimes they added different kinds of bark, herbs, or roots to the coals—that produces smoke, which cures and flavors the meat. They made fish cakes from the dried fish, and these were stored for the winter.

It was a fun game, chasing those fish into the traps. The rich rewards came in the wintertime, when they had fish for food. During the Season of the Clacking Stones, they were in their wigwams and watched their grandmothers, mothers, and sisters preparing the fish cakes. The little ones felt vital and a part of that family. They knew they had helped get those fish by chasing them into the traps. There was also a ceremony giving thanks for the fish, because they were considered a blessing. So these were all lessons contributing to their education. That's just one example of the many village activities the children were engaged in. It's a learning process: it's fun, there's ceremony, there's food, there's cooperation, respect for the teachings, and respect for all that Nature provided.

*Those families became strong and unified, because those seasonal activities involved the children from an early age.*

Many activities were designed for groups, and some were designed for individuals. There were many activities for girls, but for now, I'll just talk about the boys' education. Boys went into the forest alone to observe Nature and test their skills. Young boys had to learn hunting and fishing skills. They learned how to track and find out where different animals were at certain times of the day and season. They were shown how to make traps and snares. They had to learn those skills at an early age to be providers for when they got older and had their own families. The sooner they went off into the forests, streams, and creeks to learn their skills, the sooner they were able to be providers. If a young person was interested in a particular animal and studied it, but could not understand something that was taking place, he could turn to the elders to gain that understanding. The elders had learned and experienced many things over the generations. They were highly respected and were always there to answer questions, but the young ones were encouraged to find the answers on their own first. They were given ceremonies by the tribe for their special accomplishments while growing and learning.

Lenape boys and girls were considered adults at the age of 14 because they had learned how to act as adults and had taken a Vision Quest. The boys learned how to track game and gather the right materials to make all the various tools they needed. They mastered the craft of making and using the tools necessary to become expert hunters and fishermen. They were very capable at 14 and were ready to start looking for a mate. These same principles also applied to girls; they had to learn the skills needed to be wives and mothers, so at that same age they were also prepared.

*The rest of the time there was such abundance, it was just a matter of harvesting and giving thanks.*

## The Vital Role of Women

The women ran the household pretty much the same as modern women do. The wigwam was the household I am referring to.

It is the women who bring forth new life. They held consultations with the young girls to teach them what was involved with giving birth and motherhood. They taught the girls everything they had to know to be a good wife and mother. As mothers, they took care of rearing the children as well as the children's health and welfare.

The women were responsible for butchering the animals brought in by the hunters, food preparation, and cooking the meals. They were in charge of gathering various roots and plants for food and medicines. They planted and harvested the garden. They prepared and stored food for the winter. They prepared the hides for clothing and made all the clothing for the family. They mastered various crafts such as pottery, basketry, dyeing, and

sewing porcupine quills and feather quillwork for the decoration of moccasins, clothing, and bags. Their designs and colors were inspired by Nature. Women had organizations like today's guilds to pass on these skills to the young girls. Men and women wore ornaments they crafted from stones, bones, shells, animal claws, bird quills, and porcupine quills. Sometimes they wore bracelets, necklaces, and belts make from wampum beads. Children followed in the same dress as the parents.

In the Lenape Indian world, women carried a lot of political power. Just to give you an idea of how powerful it was, when young people married, the man went and lived with his wife's people. All the children from that marriage took on the mother's clan, not the man's. So, if you were of the Wolf Clan (Munsee) and I married you, I would move into your village or amongst your people. Our children would not be Gilberts of the Unami Clan; they would become the Gilberts of the Munsee Clan.

Now, there are some real spiritual things involved here. The Creator gave the obligation to reproduce to the female of all species, be it animal, human, plant, bird, fish, or insect. To bring forth new life is an awesome, sacred responsibility. Without the woman, or the female, all life ceases.

*So, from the Creator's position of putting the woman in this category, we understand that she is a very special person.*

She is the *most* important person, because only *she* can bring forth new life. After she brings forth new life, it is the female who does the instructing for all those early years. So women were not only powerful, they were highly revered, almost held sacred.

The Clan Mothers played a big role in selecting our chiefs. It could be that the standing chief became too old to carry on, so they met to discuss who could be the next chief responsible for the safety and well-being of the tribe. The older chief became a grandfather to the whole tribe who was honored for his experience and wisdom. It wasn't a popularity contest, or that one family had more power than another. This was not a position that was sought, or campaigned for, like with today's politicians. We only put someone in a leadership position who had shown true leadership qualities. Being a leader is a very serious position. The people knew everyone from childhood on up. In most cases, they knew the person intimately; they knew who they were and what they stood for.

When they selected a leader, it was based on the qualities that ensured the survival of the tribe. Again, clear thinking and sound judgment was on top of the list. Generosity was also very important.

The women did not want to send their sons to war, so they tried to keep things peaceful. The Clan Mothers selected the Peace Chiefs. The key to resolving disputes between tribes was the influence of the Clan Mothers and their Peace Chiefs. However you word it, it's crucial because it shows the drastic difference between modern society and traditional Lenape culture. Hopefully, modern people can relate to our traditional way of life.

The vital role of the women continued until reservation life, and then the roles changed. When Indians were put on reservations, the U.S. government insisted that the men do all the farming, whereas before it was the women who planted and harvested. When the roles were reversed, it upset a system that had been in existence for generations; a system where women had more respect and political power. That caused conflict, which has continued to present day. It's not the same now; women do not carry the same position they used to. Generally speaking, they are respected, but not to the degree that they were before. Our people have had to fit into the hodgepodge of the dominant culture. I believe that today there is not a lot of difference between the Indian and non-Indian when it comes to the roles of the man and the woman.

## The Respected Role of Men

The men were the ones who did the hard and laborious tasks such as gathering the posts, the bark, and building the wigwams. They felled trees and prepared the gardens. That may consist of burning a new area and preparing the soil for crops. To prepare the soil, they loosened up the ground with a digging stick for individual plants. They constructed dugout canoes. They built the sweat lodges. They were the hunters and trappers. In travel, their main function was to protect the travelers. They taught the young boys how to make and use all the hunting tools such as bows, arrows, arrowheads, tomahawks, knives, spears, awls, snares, and traps. The tools were made from wood, bone, stone, hide, sinew, and feathers. They taught them all the hunting and trapping skills. They taught them the skills of tracking and stalking and how to identify various animals. Understanding the habits of the animals and where they would be at certain times of the day and season was important. A lot of their hunting skills were required to be able to successfully ambush the animals. Other times they stalked the animal, which involved stealth. Both required extreme patience.

*They taught the young boys and girls to take only what they needed from Nature.*

Cleanliness was something that was stressed, and it was important to make sure their physical bodies were always in a healthy state. The men taught the boys various sports, such as swimming, running, and wrestling, to build endurance and strength.

Generally, it was a man's role to be the chief. The tribal chief put the people first, not just his family; he put the village and tribe first. The rewards were not monetary like today. Being honored by his people was the reward. He still had to acquire his family's food and daily needs. Above all, our leaders were a different kind of leader than we find in many cases today. *Clear thinking, generosity, and putting the people first were the leadership qualities they sought.* When the people in the tribe elected leaders, they knew they had selected the best. Now, not every village had a chief. But every village had headmen who were the elders and trusted decision makers. If there was a chief elected by consent, he would be a leader of several or more villages covering a wide area. It would be like a confederation today.

## The Dugout Canoe

We used wooden dugout canoes primarily for fishing and sometimes for travel. We used them in the lakes, bays, creeks, and rivers. Dugout canoes were sometimes used to reach the large schools of fish in the bays. They could carry a lot of fish. Those schools didn't always come close to shore, so we had to paddle out to them. One method we used in the creeks and rivers at night was to attract the fish with fire. We tied a torch on the front of the canoe and drifted along. The person in the front stood and speared the fish as they came to the surface, drawn in by the torch.

Those dugout canoes were durable and lasted a long time. The construction of the dugout canoe required a lot of time and effort. Because we had time and patience, only a stone axe and fire were required. The principle trees we used were cedar and tulip poplar. We planned ahead when we needed a canoe. Once a tree was selected, we gave an offering and a prayer to give thanks to the tree for sacrificing its life. Then we removed the bark around the entire base of the tree with a stone axe. This stopped the flow of sap to the tree. After one or two seasons, the tree was dried out and ready for making into a dugout canoe.

Felling those trees was done by applying fire at the base. As charcoal formed, we used a stone gouge to carve it out of the tree, then applied more fire, and gouged out more charcoal, until the tree was felled. Then, we used fire and mud to remove the interior of the

tree. The same method was used: first fire to charcoal, then gouge out the charcoal. We put mud where we didn't want the fire to burn through. That process continued until the interior of the canoe was dug out. Then we used rough stones to smooth out the interior.

My brother Jim Three Buck and I made one of those dugout canoes back in the early 1980s. One spring day, while I was roaming around the Powhatan Renape Reservation, I came across a big tulip poplar tree that had blown over in a windstorm. As I walked past it, I could visualize a dugout canoe in that tree. It was in an area that was inaccessible. I mentioned the tree to the groundskeeper, whose name was Lone Eagle.

He said, "Let's take a walk and look at it." They had just acquired one of those Kubota® tractors. He looked at the tree and said, "I believe I can get that tractor in here." He snaked it in and finally got close enough. I cut the section we would use, and he chained it to the bucket and snaked it out. He placed it in the area I was going to set up my program so I could work on it.

The understanding I want to relate here, is that it was a tree that had blown over during the winter, and it was just lying there. This tree was still green, but in the past we used a dead, standing tree because fire works better on it than a green tree. As far as length, I can only talk about the one my brother and I made, which was about 12 feet long. I don't believe it was common to make them much longer in southern New Jersey for the creeks and streams. The last I heard, it was in the museum up on the reservation.

The size of the waterway and the purpose would determine the length of the canoe they used. On occasion, dugout canoes were used to cross the Delaware River from New Jersey to places like Woodland Beach, Delaware, and vice versa. Those canoes would be longer

because it is a large body of water and it would require more paddlers. Navigating a dugout canoe can be tricky. There's no keel, so controlling direction in currents is difficult; we had to switch the paddle from side to side. It was easier with two or three paddlers in swift water. When fishing in the creeks or in the lakes, we usually just had one or two paddlers; the one who paddled in the back stayed there during the trip. The one in the front put the paddle down to spear the fish.

## Gardening the Forest

Fire was used to clear brush and fell trees to prepare new areas for farming. This would open up the forest so sunlight could reach the growing areas. The potash from the fire helped rejuvenate and fertilize the land. Those gardens were in use for quite a while before they were depleted. When a garden put too much pressure on the area's resources, the Lenape started a new one in another area. That gave the first garden a chance to rejuvenate. When they moved, they had to make burns to prepare new areas for gardens. If it was a larger group, they might also have to add an area for their wigwams. Burning was mainly for farming. The size of the burn depended on how many people were involved in the new area.

You may have heard the expression "The Three Sisters." The Three Sisters was a very effective gardening method. Corn, squash, and beans were planted together. We call them the three sisters because they are so compatible with each other. What one takes from the soil the other puts back. The bean vine climbs the corn stalk for support and supplies nitrogen to the corn and squash. The squash covers the ground and keeps it shaded and moist. I have heard that all three together make a complete protein.

I've seen in books and films where beautiful Indian gardens were portrayed with the corn planted in straight rows in uniform, military precision. That was usually not the case: many of the gardens still had stumps in them and the plantings were staggered. During a rainfall, water covered the whole area. With military-style rows, the water had a way of being channeled off. But when the plants were staggered, there was an opportunity for complete absorption of the water. I believe some tobacco was grown, but it could also be obtained through trade with the Powhatan Indians from Virginia.

**Food Preparation and Storage**

The principle garden foods were corn, squash, beans, and sunflower seeds. Our meat came from deer and smaller animals like rabbits and squirrels. We also hunted and trapped beavers, muskrats, turkeys, geese, ducks, quails, partridges, and pigeons. Most of the meat was dried, smoked or jerked and put away for winter, along with nuts and acorns.

Freshwater mussels were in abundance and available year round near the villages. Fish, clams, and oysters harvested at the coast were prepared there and transported to the winter camps and villages. Those foods would keep well into spring. With most of the tribes, there was very little left past spring.

In the spring, the Lenape dried the fish they harvested over hot oak embers on drying racks. Sometimes they added different kinds of bark, leaves, and roots to the embers, which produced smoke to help cure and flavor the meat. The dried fish was ground into flour by pounding it with stones, formed into cakes by hand, and stored. When they wanted to eat those cakes, they baked them on hot coals and poured maple syrup over them.

Deer meat that was dried on racks was put away as jerky for storage and transport. Some of that jerky would later be added to stews. In the wintertime, they pounded fat and dried berries into the deer jerky to make pemmican. Pounding softens and breaks the jerky into fibers and mixes everything together. It's a special nutritious Indian food for the winter and for travel. It does not require fire to prepare; it is ready to eat and very tasty. Acorns were a plentiful and nutritious food source. The bitter taste was leached out with water using a grass filter. Acorns were dried, stored, ground-up, and put into stews and soups. They were also ground into flour, used as cereal, and made into different kinds of bread. The acorn flour was mixed with nuts and dried berries to make muffins. Acorns stored well and were an important winter food. Acorns were also an important food source for deer, squirrels, and turkeys. Bird meat was roasted, put in stews, and also dried for storage. Sunflower seeds were eaten raw for a snack, and they were also parched and ground-up for hot cereal.

Sometimes, when a severe winter extended past the normal time, things got a little serious because food supplies could run low or even run out. When the tribe found their food supply being depleted, the headmen of each village turned to their best hunters and trappers. They asked them if they could get something that would carry the village through the rest of the winter. One of the animals they hunted at this time was the bear. It could supply a lot of meat, and the hide was good for clothing and blankets. It was very risky going after the bear, but it was the one animal that could provide enough meat for stews that would carry them through until the weather broke.

There was always a pot of stew on the fire, or close at hand, especially during the colder months. Stews were made out of roots, herbs, different meats, corn, squash, and beans.

Fish also went into the pot. We ate a lot of fish soups and chowders. Behind the eye socket on many fish is a little chunk of gristle. In it are all kinds of good minerals and vitamins. They plucked that out and it went into the stewpot. We made one meal from corn and beans called succotash. That was a staple amongst the Lenape and Algonquin tribes along the Eastern Seaboard. It's still a popular dish. Today, where people might put bacon or salt pork in, the Lenape put the whole fish head in, because there's a lot of meat on a fish's head. We used almost any kind of fish. Weakfish was a favorite with the Lenape. Down in Maryland and Delaware they call them sea trout. There's a lot of meat on that head and a lot of flavor in the eyes. Remember, we didn't waste much. In the wintertime, we used animal meat and put corn in that stew along with roots and herbs. Bear stew was a favorite. Deer, rabbits, squirrels, and raccoons were also used for stews. Stew was cooked in a good-sized clay pot that had a lip around the top. Some were flat bottomed and some were pointed on the bottom. Usually, it was either on the fire or the coals. If people stopped in to visit, food was always available.

As a holdover from way back, in the wintertime my Aunt Bess always had a pot of stew on the wood stove. When I was a kid that was something I looked forward to after coming back from hunting the Woodbury Creek area. It was usually dark and cold by the time I reached her house. From a distance, I could see the light from an oil lamp in her window. I remember coming into that warm kitchen with a fire in the wood stove and the good smell of homemade stew in the air. Aunt Bessie, who was not actually related to the family, had everything in the pot: sweet potatoes, turnips, white potatoes, carrots, potherbs, and the rabbits and squirrels that I brought her. Pheasants, which were rare, were reserved for Sunday afternoon at home.

The Lenape people dug pits and stored food underground. Storage pits were lined with limbs and branches and were used repeatedly. Corn, acorns, nuts, and seeds were easy to store in those pits. Meat that was dried and smoked, such as jerky and pemmican, was placed in rawhide containers and stored in those pits. They selected areas for storage on high ground with sandy soil. Today, archaeologists and anthropologists are finding those pits, and they can tell which pits had been opened and closed, sometimes many times, by the different colored layers of soil. They have found storage pits that still contain some of those preserved foods—the food stored that well. If the people found an area with plenty of resources that was convenient to the village, they built and maintained those pits for generations.

I've only seen one storage pit. It was found in Dover, Delaware, at Hickory Bluff. A highway called Scarborough Road was going to built nearby. When they were excavating, they discovered indications of a Lenape village. The dig was near a patch of woods. About two or three miles away, they found two storage pits. Cara Bloom, an archaeologist I know, called me to help identify them. I'm sure they knew what those pits were all about, but I think they just wanted some Indian input. Let me describe the terrain: it was high ground with sandy soil that sloped down to what was once a clear running stream that fed into Silver Lake about a mile away. The trees there were all nut trees: hickory, walnut, oak, and probably chestnut trees (before the chestnut blight). This is the area where they gathered and stored acorns and other nuts. Each village usually had its own storage area, but sometimes groups shared the same area. The location might be so agreeable that other groups also had their pits there. We never had any conflicts with that arrangement.

## The Bow and the Arrow

The role of a hunter was extremely important to the man and his tribe. The making of a bow is very carefully done. It begins with knowing what kinds of wood make the best bows. Some wood is much better than others. Top of the line is Osage orange; it is a durable wood with a very close grain, so it's very springy. Osage orange originally came from areas that became Texas and southwestern Arkansas. That is where the Osage Indian people lived. When the wood is first harvested, it has an orange cast. Up in the northern part of the state of Delaware, on the old farms, you will see a light green and chartreuse colored, bumpy fruit called the hedge apple. It's the fruit of the Osage orange tree. Over a period of time, the European colonials planted the thorny tree here in the East as a hedge around their farms. The next best wood is hickory, then oak, ash, and cedar. I don't put cedar near the top, but it makes a pretty good bow. I have made bows out of sassafras, but I put that at the bottom of the list.

When I make a bow, I seek out a particular sapling: I try to find one in an area where it didn't get a lot of sunlight. This tree had to struggle to get to the light, and in many cases it

wasn't going to make it anyway. If it did, it wouldn't be straight because of the other trees around it. Other times, I will select one that hasn't gone all through that process. When I harvest a sapling, I make a tobacco offering. For anything as serious as taking a life, the tobacco offering is the way I express appreciation. It's a prayer, thanking the Creator for bringing that tree into life. I ask forgiveness of the tree for taking its life. Then, I have a moment of silence to slow everything down, to show my thankfulness. The tobacco is a gift to the tree, to the soil, and to Mother Earth. It's a sacred offering that's been given to us by the Creator.

I put the saplings I harvest up in the rafters of the basement. If I have time, I will leave them there all winter long, or even a year or two. When the wood is dried and cured, I start to cut the wood down to the size and shape that I want. I don't rush. Anytime I make something—especially a bow—I try to do the best I can. That's an extension of me, especially for an article I would use to survive by. I don't put a time limit on myself because then I may rush and not do my best. Here in the East, the Lenape bows were straight and fairly long compared to the bows of the Plains Indians, which were short reinforced bows. The Plains Indians were buffalo hunters; the buffalo hunters on horseback needed short, powerful bows. They used sinew to reinforce their bows. It was applied to the front part to give it additional strength.

Many different types of wood are used for arrow shafts, including cedar, hickory, oak, wild rose, and arrowwood. Today, I use the butterfly bush because in the early winter I have to prune mine. They make excellent arrows. However, oak is the best wood I have found to make arrow shafts. If you have ever been in the woods after a winter windstorm, you might see where a young oak tree has broken off. Those splinters that stick up make excellent arrows. It's a lot of work to get them down to the diameter I want, but they are shafts that never have to be reshaped. Other types of wood may warp, and we have a method for getting that warp out. It's done with heat and what we call arrow wrenches made from deer leg bones drilled with holes. I put one on each end of the shaft. I hold the part of the shaft that I need to straighten over hot coals from an oak fire until the wood becomes hot to the touch. Then I take either deer or bear fat and rub it on the heated area I want to straighten. I hold it over the hot coals again and the heat starts to make the fat soften and bubble. It will be absorbed into the wood. Then I straighten the shaft and hold it out in the cool air, and when it cools, it stays straight. That's one of the ways to straighten arrows.

Turkey feathers were used for arrow fletching, which helps the arrow fly straight to its target. For the fletching on my arrows, I use wild turkey feathers. They are stiff and they hold up pretty good. There are several methods of attaching the feathers. One is to tie the ends of the cut feathers, but that is not as secure a method. I use glue and tying; that way I've got a double whammy. The old way was to use hide glue. It was made from the inner membrane of the deer's hide, crushed deer toes, cut-up sinew, and chopped-up rawhide. We mixed that all together with water and cooked it. As it cooked down, it became the consistency of porridge. It was equivalent to modern man's wood glue. So again, every part of the deer was used, and glue was one of the important uses for those parts. Every part of the wild turkey was used. The wings were made into fans and headdresses.

For the arrow points, many types of stone were used. Flint was a big item and so was jasper. They both are fairly easy to work and are durable. One of the areas to get jasper is in northern Delaware behind the Iron Hill Museum, where there were jasper pits. Jasper was a trade item in New Jersey and Pennsylvania. Cohansey quartzite was found near the Cohansey River in southern New Jersey. It is a durable material, but it's more difficult to work.

Obsidian is found in areas that had volcanic action. Another name for it is volcanic glass. It's easy to work and super sharp, but it's fragile. Obsidian came to the Lenape from tribes in the Rocky Mountains. Those tribes travelled to rendezvous locations where many tribes came to trade. Then the obsidian continued on to rendezvous locations further east. Trade could only take place if there were peaceful relations, and before European contact, trade flowed freely throughout the land.

The Lenape developed the skills to work the stone. They shaped and sharpened the stone by knapping and pressure flaking. First, the piece was shaped (or knapped) by striking it with a hammerstone, or the base of an antler. Then they put on a piece of brain-tanned deerskin cut to fit in the palm of their hand. The stone was held with their fingers against their palm and then the sharp point of a deer antler was used to chip off flakes of stone. It's called pressure flaking. Once they got a leading edge, they applied pressure at the correct angle and a flake came off. The angle and motion will determine the size and shape of the flake. They continued that until they got the correct shape with sharp edges and points. The person who specialized in making arrow points, shafts, and bows could trade those items with the hunters. If a hunter didn't quite have the skills to make the best bow or arrows and wanted to use the best, he supplied the bow maker with meat from the hunts in exchange for a bow and arrows.

### Tribal Colors / Personal Colors

The arrow is an extension of the person who makes it. With my tribe, every young boy was taught how to make an arrow, what materials are best, and the significance of the colors. Sometimes, you may see a western movie with John Wayne, and he will come riding up to a covered wagon that's overturned with arrows stuck in the side. He will pull out an arrow and look at it and say, "Well, that arrow came from a Cheyenne Dog Soldier."

With many North American tribes, we could tell what tribe the arrow belonged to by the various colors or markings on it. Here, along the Eastern Seaboard, the Lenape colors are red, green, and yellow. They're not always in a certain order, but those three colors will be together. That indicates it's a Lenape arrow.

Then we have our individual markings. The purpose of the individual markings is this: if there is a communal hunt, and maybe it takes three arrows to kill the deer, the hunters look at the arrow closest to the heart to see whose arrow it is. That hunter gets the choice portions of the deer and has the honor of providing the elders with the tender tongue, heart, and liver, all easy to digest.

Now, with my arrows, I have the yellow, the red, and the green, which indicates it's a Lenape arrow. For my personal markings, the colors are black, yellow, red, and white. These indicate the four races side by side, as I believe the Creator has meant for us to live. They represent the four races in harmony with each other. The colors are not always in that order, but those four colors together are my individual colors.

*When you look at my arrows and you see those colors together, I want you to remember that I consider everyone as brothers and sisters.*

Now, some have told me that's a very naive view, and it very well might be, but why not entertain that view? Why not have this view, that we are all brothers and sisters? Isn't that better than *not* being brothers and sisters? Maybe there are people who say: "Well, that makes more sense." Instead of me hating this guy, I'm going try to love him, and that, in a sense, is helping to fulfill the teachings of Jesus. I'm sure this world would be a whole lot better if people had this view instead of beating up on each other. Again, it might be a very naive way of looking at it, but let's look anyway.

## Tribal Justice

Remember the expression “honest Injun?” You don’t hear it anymore. People who don’t know take it as some kind of joke. But it was no joke.

Lying was a mortal sin! The Lenape learned that early in life. Lying put a person in jeopardy because nobody could trust him. If someone were caught in a deliberate lie, he was banished from the tribe and the village. The village leaders (usually the elders) made that decision. Runners were sent to the other villages to inform them that this person was a liar. He was a lost fawn in the high weeds because nobody would have anything to do with him. If he came into another village, they banned him. He was left adrift to travel the woods the rest of his life alone. The punishment for stealing from a tribal member was also banishment, and automatic. It was a very rare occurrence.

Those laws were so essential that the people lived by them. Everything was honored. Everything took place within the Creation and was witnessed by Creation. A lie upset tribal relations and, in a sense, dishonored Creation. Those tribal laws had to be very strict. Do you remember they had that honor system at West Point? Well, this was very similar, only the honor was not just amongst the people; that honor went through all of Creation.

My father used to talk about a man’s word. He said, “A man’s word is his bond, and if the man’s word is no good, then the man is no good.” In many cases, no one would have anything to do with that person. He said that person had to go to another town because no one would deal with him: his word was no good.

Being banned was a harsh punishment because it meant the man would be alone. His family could not go with him. It made no difference what his position was. His name was no good, and he was going to roam the forest alone. It’s similar to the boy who cried wolf, where the people couldn’t trust him—he was not trustworthy. Living under tribal circumstances, peer pressure was very much in force amongst the people. You couldn’t be walking around with something negative like that hanging on you, plus you would be disgracing your family. It’s just a terrible thing. The worst punishment was to be separated from your family and tribe. Tribal laws were strict, but lasted so long because the family and the tribe was your whole life.

The people had been taught at a very early age not to lie and what the consequences were, so by the age of 14 they knew the laws. It was not a thing where someone could say, "I didn't know." Everyone knew, and that was why it rarely happened. We didn't step outside of those laws because we knew they were there to protect everyone. If you broke them, you didn't fit. Once that word got out, even tribes that were not friendly couldn't trust you either. If you got too close to their territory, you would be in jeopardy.

The Lenape were people who enjoyed each other's company. They were tribal people, social people, and to be alone was a situation they could not imagine. I've seen programs on TV about wolves, and they'll talk about a lone wolf and how its chances for survival are diminished. That must be a terrible circumstance to find yourself in. One of the problems of today is that a person can break man-made laws and move down to the next state. You see, that wasn't the circumstance back then. When you broke those laws in a village, it stayed with you wherever you went. You couldn't get away with it like you can today.

The chief and the elders were people of high honor and we would strive for that kind of honor. They were the role models; we sought to be like them. Children grew up wanting to be like their role models. Why destroy your honor? I remember people talking about my father—what an honest man he was, and a good man. We were poor, but I remember those old timers back then. They could look at you and tell what family you came from. There was a certain resemblance.

If you were Harry Gilbert's son, oh man, you were "in like Flynn." Harry Gilbert gave all of his children birth marks. On the back of our heads we all have the same red birth mark.

## What Time Is It?

We looked at life in an entirely different way. European time was one of the hardest things for Indian people to adapt to.

You may have heard me speak of "Indian time." We didn't measure time the way the Europeans do. We measured time by the seasons. The tribes came together for trade, ceremonies, treaties, or other occasions. Generally speaking, a season comes about at different times for each tribe due to the geographical features and location of their village as well as their local weather patterns. We might say it will be during the Season of the

Berry-Picking Moon, which indicated June.

So, as long as we got there around that time period, it was okay. We had a very casual attitude when it came to time. It didn't have the same implications for us as it did for the Europeans.

Here in the East, if the Europeans were supposed to meet with the people at a certain location at 8:00 in the morning and the people didn't show up, they thought the Indians had a problem. The Lenape people might leave around noontime and the Europeans got very upset with them because they were not adhering to the European standard of time. Indian people just couldn't understand that. We didn't have a word for time in the European sense.

Well, after I retired from the workforce, one of the first sets of shackles I wanted to get off of me was time. Time was something I knew I had to track when I was in the workforce to take care of my family, but outside of that, I wasn't going to let time be that compelling. I'll see people rushing even when they don't need to because they've gotten caught up in this time thing. Everything is rush, rush, rush. I resist that. Once I got those shackles off, I thought: I am not going to let time have that kind of power over me anymore. Yet, I have still managed to be a part of modern society. Some will say: "Well, you should have been here at 8:00," and I might get there by 8:30. It's just that maybe that morning I felt like having an extra cup of coffee, or maybe I just wanted to linger in the backyard a little longer. I like the idea that this time system has not locked me in.

My Uncle Copper always said nerves could kill you quicker than anything. He had complete control over his nerves; he took his time with everything.

I don't wear a watch. I haven't worn a watch since I was in the Air Force. That was back in the 1950s. I've always managed to be on time for work, and I've always managed to leave work on time. They were the only two times that were important to me.

### Wampum and Trade

Wampum beads were made from the purple and white parts of the quahog clam shell. The craftsman used a very simple hand drill to make beads from the shells. If you see one, you would wonder how in the world they did it; it was very difficult. Only special craftsmen did this; there's a lot of work involved. They used flint or jasper for the drill bit. The craftsman had to start with a big piece of shell to drill the hole. Once he got the hole through, he had to take that shell and rub it and grind it down on a braiding stone to get it down to the right size and shape to be sewn onto an animal pelt. A braiding stone is kind of a rough stone, and as the shell was rubbed on it, the shell broke down to a chalk-like powder until the bead was finished.

Contrary to what the history books say, we did not use wampum as money. The Europeans used it as money, because the wampum beads were rare. When they came here, they had very little in the way of coin money, so they used our wampum as money. Sometimes we used it in trade, but its principle use was to record events. We sewed wampum beads on deerskin to make symbols and pictographs. The pictographs signified certain events, such as an agreement or treaty. It was equivalent to a legal contract. They were also used to record unusual events in Nature, such as hurricanes or floods.

Wampum beads were sewn into specific images to describe an event. If two tribes came together to form a treaty, they used wampum beads to create images on a deerskin to symbolize that agreement. Using symbols with wampum beads was their form of writing. Those beads were also used to make wampum belts. Those belts also represented contracts, agreements, or treaties, especially between the Europeans and the Indians.

One famous belt has a pictograph of a Lenape Indian and William Penn woven into it. It shows them holding hands in friendship. It depicted the first treaty between the Lenape tribes near Philadelphia and William Penn. He was a Quaker and the founding father of Philadelphia. He was honest and fair with us. It was a treaty of friendship. The Lenape gave him the name Onas (brother).

I think most of the Lenape wampum belts have been lost. The Iroquois held on to a lot of theirs and the State of New York got a hold of many of them. Not too long ago, the Iroquois went to court and got them back. These belts are very important because they recorded the people's history, their relationship with other tribes, and their agreements with the Europeans. Wampum beads were also used for earrings, necklaces, bracelets, and things of that nature. Wood, berries, nuts, seeds, and a variety of things were also used for beads, but the shell was generally more durable. Wampum was a very important trade item because the interior Indians did not have access to clamshells. They had to come to us to trade for those wampum beads. So, if we had wampum beads, we could demand a lot in exchange. By the same token, if they had black obsidian, they could demand a lot in exchange because we could make such excellent tools with it such as arrow points, spear points, and knives.

The Shawnee people and other tribes from as far away as the Ohio country came to the Jersey Shore to trade black obsidian and other items for seafood and sometimes wampum beads.

## Disease, Guns, and Rum

One of the most devastating effects of European contact with the Lenape people was exposure to European diseases. As Europeans came to the area, the Lenape Indians were exposed to new diseases such as smallpox, measles, tuberculosis, pneumonia, and whooping cough. They were absolutely devastating to the people. While those diseases were not fatal to most Europeans, the North American Indians had no immunity. Epidemics decimated entire villages. As each outbreak took its toll, some say over 90 percent of the Lenape population died.

When the Lenape people first started to have contact with the Europeans, and the Europeans came to trade, some of the items they brought were very exciting to the people. The Lenape started to acquire metal knives and hatchets. They soon realized that metal was a lot more durable than their stone hatchets and knives and much more effective. The Lenape believed that metal was a very special thing in their lives, so at first they were eager to trade for it. For a period of time, they thought those metal tools would help their way of life. Metal hatchets made cutting trees easier and faster than fire for the men, and they were much more durable.

Then they started to trade for guns. For thousands of years they had been taught to know the animal they were hunting so well that they could stalk the animal on foot to within the range of a bow and arrow. Most of their shots were within 20 or 30 yards. They had mastered the art of camouflage, how to smother their scent, and how to stalk. Well, with the gun, they could harvest animals from a much longer distance. They started harvesting more than they normally would because the Europeans wanted those hides for trade. Deer hides were very important to the European trade system. As the hunters used those guns, they had to kill more deer because then they needed gunpowder and lead shot.

As they started to kill and destroy more, the elders in the tribe realized that this was not their way. They knew the Creator would not be pleased with this destruction. So, for a period of time, they forbade the young hunters and trappers to trade with the Europeans. Europeans came into the village to trade, and there was no trade. They had been taught for generations to never take more than they needed from the Natural World.

The elders advised the people not to use the metal hatchets because it was too easy to over-harvest, which would upset Nature's balance. Their traditional stone tools allowed them to take just what they needed and no more.

Then, an enterprising young European realized that if they made a hatchet that also served as a pipe, it was two things in one. They presented that hatchet/pipe for trade, and even though some of the young trappers and hunters liked this idea, there was still no trade. That's when the Europeans began to ply the young braves with rum. Rum undermined the whole tribal system. With rum, the braves began to disrespect the elders and each other. When the Europeans realized that rum was destroying our whole way of life, they applied more rum. It was very effective. It eventually caused the Lenape people to be displaced from their homes in the forest on the Eastern Seaboard. So disease, guns, and rum played a big role in the displacement and the downfall of the Lenape people. As they were forced further and further away from the coast, the Europeans moved in to occupy their traditional homelands.

I believe the Lenape were so susceptible to alcohol because for thousands of years their systems had never had been exposed to it. Now, take into consideration this was at a time when we could freely drink from almost any body of water. The water was pure and the air was fresh. The people lived outdoors most of their lives and they wore few clothes

(except in the winter) so their bodies could breathe. The food they ate was natural and high in fiber. The medicines they used were natural. They were a physical people and spiritually connected to the Mother Earth. Alcohol was foreign to their systems, so it had a devastating effect. It was easy for them to become addicted to alcohol and their addiction accelerated their downfall.

## Going Back in Time

My Uncle Copper had a picture of a painting hung on his bedroom wall. I remember going upstairs sometimes just to sit there and study that picture. It was fascinating to me.

In that picture is a young Indian boy about the age of ten sitting in a wigwam. There is a fire, and a water jug made from clay, and a tripod with a deerskin stretched on it. An older Indian is sitting on a coyote skin, painting images on the deerskin and explaining to this young Indian boy what those images represented. The picture seemed almost alive to me.

Looking at that picture, I could visualize myself back before European contact, sitting in that wigwam. My father or my uncle is painting that picture on the deerskin. This deerskin painting told a story; it has Indians on horseback and on foot. I think this fascinated me because I could feel myself going back to that time.

Uncle Copper knew that picture had a strong effect on me. When he passed on he didn't have much in the way of material possessions, but he left me that picture and his pocketknife. I felt proud that he had left that picture to me. It's a connection to him and to the past. There are very few things that can send me back to the old ways and the old times like that picture. It has a soothing effect on me. Today, that picture hangs in my den.

*It helps me start my day by remembering who I am, where I am, and why I am.* They were the good times, a simple way of life and a very good way. A Ho Ka!

When I was growing up, there was a field of Indian grass about a mile from our house. It's a reddish grass with a thin stalk about the thickness of a broom straw. It might have gotten its name because of the coppery color. It grows about three feet high and is beautiful to see with the wind blowing through it. My brothers, Ralph and Jim, had built a wigwam about halfway between the creek and home in a grove of tree saplings. I remember this because it left a strong impression on me. The frame was made from gum saplings, which they bent over and tied into a dome shape. Saplings were encircled around the dome frame like ribs. Then they covered this frame with Indian grass. They tied the grass in clumps. When we came from the creek, we usually stopped-over in this wigwam. We relaxed and reflected on the day's hunt and sometimes planned the next day's hunt. It was our cool-out time.

I remember coming back from the creek cold and wet after duck hunting or trapping. I knew that when I got to the wigwam, I could get comfortable and warm up; that was my little sanctuary.

For two or three years before they built up the area, I maintained and repaired our wigwam. It was a way station, just like in the old days. My people had areas where they rested after hunting along the creek before they journeyed to the main camp. Maybe they took a nap, or if the weather turned bad, stayed until the weather cleared up. It was a little place to go and relax, and as I got older, I spent a lot of time there. It was always a very soothing, reflective time.

It was a sacred place for me because it was like going back in time and living the old ways—*I was back those 500 years.*

When I am doing my crafts, I go both ways: sometimes I'm in the present, and sometimes I'm in the past. When I'm working the clacking stones, I often think about my grandsons, Avery and Tyler, and how I'll explain to them how this tool will look when it's finished and what it will be used for. It will be a teaching time. I will describe what materials they will need and where to find them. This is a throwback to a time when these teaching events took place during the season of the clacking stones.

Making these crafts is my way of reaching back. A lot of imagination goes into my handcrafting. When I'm seeking to represent something in the design with colors and patterns, I'll sometimes glean from the past. I try to imagine what a Lenape Indian of old would use on that tool to indicate something special or give it significance.

*By working the stone and thinking about these things, I can get so absorbed that I sometimes step through the present and into the past.*

## A Tale of Two Peoples

There was a custom that existed for many generations with the Lenape peoples of New Jersey and Delaware.

In Kent County, Delaware, there is a place called Woodland Beach. It sits right on the Delaware River. Directly across the river in New Jersey lies the hamlet of Greenwich. From that area, many of the Lenape people from New Jersey traveled by dugout canoes across the Delaware River to Woodland Beach. On that day, the Lenape groups from New Jersey and Delaware came together for ceremonies, dancing, and a big feast. That was an opportunity for young people to meet. The Delaware girls had a reputation for being very beautiful, and the Delaware boys felt the same way about the Lenape girls from New Jersey.

In modern times, this custom was called Woodland Beach Day. Many marriages came about because of Woodland Beach Day. I remember my mother telling me about going across in her cousin's boat. That event existed for a very long time—nobody knows how long. Well, that custom faded out in the early 1950s. There were two devastating hurricanes in that area, and it took a long time for the community to recover. In the meantime, the custom ceased.

I had a very good occasion with Avery when he was four years old. I took him to Woodland Beach, and we walked along gathering pebbles and shells. Afterword, we sat down facing the river to the Jersey side. I asked him if he could see trees on that side of the river. It's very wide there and I wasn't sure if he could see them; he told me he could. I commenced to tell him about the history of Woodland Beach and its relationship to the Lenape Indian people on the other side of the river. I told him the story of how our people came across the river by dugout canoes, and later by boats, to Woodland Beach. I described how those Lenape families from the Delaware side greeted them. I told him how they had ceremonies, feasts, and danced, and that it was a good time. I felt grateful that I was able to sit there on that beach feeling the breeze from the river and telling him the story of our two peoples. I felt privileged that I could pass on that kind of knowledge and information to my grandson.

I hope that one day in his life he'll be able to do the same—to sit there with his grandson or granddaughter and tell them the history of our people, and how we came together in unity at Woodland Beach. A Ho Ka!

# 5.
# SEASONS AND CEREMONIES

*"My people lived in accordance with the seasons. Generally speaking, seasons came about at different times for each tribe due to the geographical features and location of their villages as well as their local weather patterns." -Chief Quiet Thunder*

## Sensing Spring

The cardinal sings his spring song in the late winter. His song creates vibrations all across the land. Those vibrations bring on the March winds, and the March winds bring the April showers. As the rain falls upon Mother Earth and reawakens the earthworms, they come to the surface—this brings the robins back to the land. When the robins return we hear their beautiful singing in the morning. This alerts our sense of hearing. The songs of the robin bring the spring flowers. The brilliance of the colors heightens our sense of sight, and the flowers bring the fragrance. The fragrance of the flowers alerts our sense of smell.

*Then, we touch the Earth and feel its awesome power.* My grandmother used to say that in the morning when you walk barefoot on the dew-covered grass, you can feel the power coming up from the Earth. These are just some of the gifts the Creator has given us. We can appreciate all these gifts because we've been given our physical senses.

*We connect to the Living World through our senses. A Ho Kah!*

Each season was an *event* where there was either harvesting or planting and a celebration to follow. The celebration involved everyone in the village and combined dancing, drumming, and a feast. This introduced the children to their culture at a young age, and they would look forward to these events every year. These events and celebrations gave them a strong connection to Mother Earth early on.

### Spring Mother Earth Reawakening: Early Spring Through Spring

In the early spring, we had the Spring Mother Earth Reawakening Celebration. In the spring, plants are turning green, the blossoms are out, and life is coming back. It is a time to celebrate. In the past, it was a celebration because we had come through another winter. Some Piscataway people still have ceremonies related to this celebration. I believe a lot of the western tribes still adhere to it. But here in the East, I don't think there are many that are even aware of it. Some still celebrate the Spring Reawakening here, but today we have a deeper sense of knowing that Mother Earth is hurting.

*There are devastating events taking place in Nature that can be directly or indirectly tied to man's tampering with Natural Laws.*

We have special dances intended to heal the wounds of Mother Earth. The ceremony, the dance, and the drumming come together to help heal the heartbeat of Mother Earth. These dances and ceremonies are based on the natural rhythms of this land and go back many generations. Being the indigenous people of this land, traditional Indian people believe that we have a *sacred obligation* to try to heal the Earth and to reach for and connect with all spirits. Our spiritualism connects us to the land and this obligation. It is also a way to show that we appreciate this land: instead of just taking it for granted, we try to connect with it. To take that further is to make non-Indian people realize that you can't always take these things for granted. Try, as we do—try to help Mother Earth and not be abusive to her.

*Do not take for granted that spring will always bring these good things to us.*

The Spring Mother Earth Reawakening Ceremony is one of the few times that I dance. Usually I am alone. This dance is to help bring balance back to Mother Earth because she is out of balance. I believe that part of the destiny of being an Indian here in North America is to help bring back that balance.

*The drumbeat is a heartbeat, and the dance is to the rhythm of the heartbeat; it is designed to spiritually heal the heartbeat of the Earth.* When I do the ceremony, I approach it with prayer, thankful that I have come through another winter.

QUIET THUNDER

My prayer goes like this:

> *Oh Creator of All Life, I thank you for all the gifts you have given me: those that I'm aware of as well as those that I'm not aware of. I thank you for these gifts. I pray that you will continue to bless me, and that I may be worthy of all these blessings.*

It's a very simple prayer, and it covers how I feel. For the second part, I try to dance that heartbeat rhythm with my feet and the drum. I believe that our prayers and beliefs are very crucial at this time. I have to be sincere. If I am performing these ceremonies and I'm not sincere in my prayers, my prayers will not be heard. That has a lot to do with why I don't perform at powwows. I reserve the ceremony and prayer strictly for myself so I don't have any interference or distractions. The prayers and everything that is done are sincere.

The drum and the sound of the drum are very natural to this land. Much of this tradition has been lost here in the East. The Plains Indians still have a mastery of what the drum and the different beats are all about. It goes all the way back to when there was nothing except for the Great Spirit, God—the Creator.

In our Creation Mythology:

> *The Great Red Cedar Tree grew from the Turtle's back. The first Lenape Man and Woman grew from the roots of that first Cedar Tree.*

We were connected to the land from the very beginning. Our existence is tied to this land we call Turtle Island. We are the land and the land is us, and our ceremonies spiritually connect us to the land. That spiritual connection doesn't diminish—it continues right up to the present day. There are many who don't realize that the spirits of their ancestors are here in this land.

*If we break that connection to the land, then we lose our spiritual connection with our ancestors.*

Here in the East, if traditional Indians perform a ceremony, they do it together without any spectators, or they do it alone. Spectators don't understand the purpose of what's taking place. They take it as entertainment, which takes away some of its spiritual power. If it's performed alone, it's more likely to be sincere. I've heard people say things at the powwows like, "Oh, that dancer is cool," or "The regalia and feathers look so colorful!" Dancing is not supposed to be taken as entertainment. It's supposed to be taken very seriously, just as the pipe is taken seriously. So many Indian people have gotten away from this, and it becomes a spectator situation.

The Spring Mother Earth Reawakening Ceremony was performed during the ripening berries and the corn planting. The Clan Mothers would determine when the celebration was held.

### The Season of the Ripening Berries: Early Spring

The Berry Season started in the early spring with the wild strawberries. Strawberry time was very special for the Lenape people. Strawberries were the first spring fruits. There's a lot of power and a lot of medicine in strawberries. The Spring Mother Earth Reawakening Season continued with the Coming of the Strawberries Ceremony. That ceremony was very important because strawberries were a spring medicine. In that ceremony, we thanked the Creator for the strawberry.

Today, in the spring, you will see signs saying: Strawberry Festival. It's usually little hamlets in the country that have those strawberry festivals. The churches that have those festivals don't really know the total history of it. So the next time you see a sign saying Strawberry Festival, remember that it stemmed from those ceremonies my people had every spring when the strawberries became ripe. The Season of the Ripening Berries included all the activities and the ceremonies that took place within that season.

## Corn-Planting Time: Early Spring

Corn-Planting Time falls along with the Spring Mother Earth Reawakening Celebration. As the Earth wakens, we start to prepare the soil for planting. The Clan Mothers and women had the responsibility to plant the corn and the gardens. It was a festive time when they got together to place seeds into Mother Earth, knowing that she is going to tenderly handle those kernels and help to bring forth the plant.

For something as important as planting corn, I'm certain there was a ceremony, but I'm not sure how that took place. As I can recall, even when I was small, this was a happy time of year, not just for planting the corn, but also for preparing the garden in general. It was a big event. When I was growing up, we didn't have the ceremony; it was just a good feeling that we knew that by late summer we were going to have some corn. I know that the Lenape used to plant corn with a fish in a small mound. They dug the hole, placed the fish in the hole, put some soil over the fish, and then planted the seed over that. As it germinated, the seed reached out for the fish, which was the fertilizer.

## The Season of the South Fish: Early Spring

This season was called the Season of the South Fish, or the Season of the Coming of the Fish.

Around what we now call April, while the Clan Mothers and women were planting the gardens and corn, many of the remaining villagers walked across the land to the Delaware River shore. This included some of the women and children. When they arrived, they harvested the migratory fish such as the shad and herring. The Lenape people referred to shad as the "south fish." We fished schools of shad, herring, white perch, and rockfish. Those fish traveled up the Delaware River and its tributaries to spawn. This was a very exciting time for us. It was also a very important time because we had to teach our young ones how to harvest those fish. The methods that we used were traps and spears (described in the story of traditional village life on page 122). The young ones who participated in planting the garden looked forward to learning how to harvest the fish the following year.

This time frame did not necessarily apply to every Lenape group. I'm talking about my group, the Unami. It pertained to a specific set of circumstances. Other groups further north or south may have a different interpretation, but we understood that. That was the case for all of the seasons and ceremonies. The migration of the shad may be different in those other areas because of the layout of the land. The migrating fish travel upriver with the tide into the streams, creeks, and tributaries. They came into Woodbury Creek before they came up Big Timber Creek. As those streams filled up, the fish kept moving further north.

### The Green Corn Festival: Midsummer

The Green Corn Festival took place in midsummer when the first ears of green corn became loaded with corn milk. During the Green Corn Festival, the first corn was given as an offering back to Mother Earth in a ceremony. With this ceremony, we thanked the Creator and Mother Earth for the corn, a very important crop. Afterwards, we had a big corn feast. Corn originally only grew in this hemisphere. It is a gift from the Creator. The Indian people, in return, have given this gift to the entire world. This ceremony varied from tribe to tribe and location to location. It was not just here in the East. This took place in most of the Indian communities who grew crops. We were recognizing this gift of corn that the Creator has given to the Indian people.

*It was very important—it still is. Corn feeds the entire world today.*

After we celebrated the Green Corn Festival, many members of my tribal group packed up and walked east to the coast to harvest the shellfish. The very young, the sick, the elderly, and anyone who was not able to make the journey, stayed behind. They tended the gardens and took care of the very young ones. So the elders, especially, were still serving the tribe in a vital way. That was very important, and it is one of the things missing now in our elder societies.

*Today, as they get older, the elderly are pushed to the side and disconnected from their families. When that happens, they no longer have a purpose in life—it's a sure road to their rapid decline.*

## The Season of the Quahog: Summer

The Season of the Quahog took place at the seashore. It was the time and place for harvesting the quahog clams and the shellfish. After the tribal group settled into their seashore camps and villages, families dug up and harvested quahogs, both for the meat and the shell. Even though the fish, crabs, and oysters were important, the quahog was the focal point. The young boys and girls also helped dig up the quahogs. We made wampum beads from the purple and white parts of the quahog shell. Wampum beads represented so much: they were a means of communication by recording the past with symbols woven into wampum belts (see: "Wampum and Trade" page 148). Wampum beads and the shell were also used as jewelry.

The Lenape used different methods for catching fish, depending on the area. Sometimes they caught fish by scouring the shore, wading in the water using spears or nets. In other areas, they constructed fish weirs or chased the fish into traps. These were built in the marshes, and in some cases, along the shore. Fish weirs were constructed by driving poles into the bottom in rows and staking them off, creating walls so the fish were not able to get out. They built those weirs in areas that still had enough water to hold fish at low tide. The size of those weirs depended on the size of the tribe and the area.

At the end of the summer, after the meat was dried and stored, the Lenape packed up the quahog shells and the rest of the harvest. Then they headed back to their villages and winter camps to hunt and trap, and to harvest the corn, squash, beans, and everything else they had planted and needed to gather.

## The Hunt and the Harvesting of the Deer: Fall

Fall was the time for the hunters and trappers to hunt the fur-bearing animals. The whitetail deer played a vital role in the Lenape way of life and provided so much for us. As the bison played a vital role with the Plains Indians, the whitetail deer played a similar role with us. The eastern woodland elk was probably also important, but I have no knowledge of that. For food, the choicest parts of the deer are the heart and the liver. The tongue was considered the best meat.

The men had to prepare themselves for the hunt, and this preparation began with fasting. Often, it was a four-day fast. As I spoke earlier, the number four played a special role. The Sweat Lodge Ceremony came next: this is a purification ceremony preparing the hunters to take a life. On the morning of the hunt, the hunter went down to the stream, washed himself with sand and water, and rubbed aromatic leaves onto his body. That helped cover his scent. Then he turned and faced east. Watching the sun rise through the trees, he raised his hands in acknowledgement of the Creator. Then he prayed:

> *Brother, forgive me, that I must take your life in order for my family to live. Each time I pass through the forest where you sacrificed your life for my family, I will stop and I will say a prayer. I will give an offering.*

Those offerings were made to honor the spirit of that animal. Sometimes the offering was corn or tobacco; sometimes it was red cedar. All are considered sacred plants.

As the hunters and trappers brought in the game that was harvested, the women and many of the elders fleshed the hides and prepared them for making various items. Everyone had a role in this.

*The hunter took the weak and the injured deer first, the ones that were not going to survive the winter.* This was similar to the way the coyotes selected their prey, which strengthened the deer herd.

Every part of the animal was used—nothing was wasted. The hide was used for moccasins, breechcloths, shirts, vests, leggings, belts, dresses, winter clothing, cradles, bedding, pipe bags, pouches, quivers, and dolls. Deer hides were also used to stalk deer and other game. Rawhide was used for containers, medicine bags, moccasin soles, rattles, drums, drumsticks, clan shields, splints, ropes, thongs, knife cases, tomahawks, armbands, belts, and glue. The brain was used for hide preparation (tanning). Sinew was used for thread, bowstrings, and glue. The bones were used for knives, arrowheads, arrow straighteners, awls, game dice, needles, deer clan symbols, hoes, and scrapers. The antlers were used for arrowhead knapping and flaking, headpieces, and moving red-hot rocks into the sweat lodge. The toes were used for ankle rattles and glue. The stomach contents were used as a poultice for frostbite treatment, and skin infections and diseases. The marrow from the bones was used like butter. The hunter wore an antler head piece and a robe made from a deer hide to imitate a deer. Even animal scent was used to attract game. Deer urine was used to attract deer to an area. The scent gland of a beaver was smeared around a trap to attract other beavers.

### The Gathering Season: Late Fall

By late fall, the Lenape were settled into their permanent camps and villages. The Gathering Season began when the leaves started to turn to their fall colors. Nature does not follow a calendar and neither did the Lenape people. "Indian time" means roundabout; the Gathering Season was around the time the leaves changed colors. There is a relationship between the nuts, herbs, berries, and roots ripening, and the leaves turning to their fall colors. This varied in different areas.

This was another exciting time. As nights grow cooler, there is urgency in the air. This

is the time to gather and harvest everything the people will need to carry them through the cold winter months. Families will soon be gathering the acorns, nuts, berries, roots, and herbs they need. Everyone participated. Also, at this time, families dug out any new storage pits they would need to store the harvest.

The hunters and trappers walked into the forests and creeks to hunt and trap. The rest of the family members went into the forest to do the gathering.

*Even the very young came along with their families to gather nuts, roots, and fruit.* They learned what to harvest, where to harvest, and the best time to harvest. Those who were too small to participate stayed in the villages with the elders. The hunt and the harvest was a learning experience and everyone contributed. There were also individual ceremonies that dealt with everything that was harvested because all those things played a part in providing for the people through the winter months.

After everything was harvested, the tribes prepared for their thanksgiving ceremonies.

**The Dance of the Deer: Season of the Touching Leaves; Late Fall**

What Europeans called Thanksgiving, the Lenape called The Deer Dance or The Dance of the Deer. By this time, the deer had been prepared and much of the meat had been smoked or jerked and put away for winter. The harvest was the culmination of all the fall hunts and gatherings, which included all the acorns, nuts, berries, and roots. It was everything we needed to carry us through the cold months.

The Dance of the Deer was a ceremony where the people gave thanks to the Creator for the deer and honored the spirit of the deer. It was a very important ceremony. The medicine person dressed up with a deerskin cape and a headpiece with deer antlers. He or she might have a wand made with a deer antler or hooves. Men and women painted their faces in

colorful designs for their festivals and ceremonial dances. Men sometimes painted their legs and chests as well. The villagers assembled in a circle around the medicine person. Dancers had deer toes tied around their ankles for rattles. Then the medicine person and the villagers danced in a circle clockwise while the medicine person chanted.

*Those chants were prayers thanking the Creator for the deer because the deer supplied so much to the people.*

Honoring the spirit of the deer was to ensure that the spirit of the deer remained there in the forest so there would be more deer. If we did not honor that spirit, the deer would disappear. *You must honor that animal.* After the ceremony, the people would have a big feast.

### The Ceremony of Mesingwe: Late Fall

The Ceremony of Mesingwe honored the spirits of all animals. The red and black mask represented Mesingwe, Spirit-Keeper of the Animals. A dancer wore the black and red mask. The identity of the dancer was kept secret. The dancer, who was probably a medicine person, wore the mask, was dressed in a bearskin robe, and shook a turtle shell rattle. The image and dance of Mesingwe appeared during the Season of the Touching Leaves along with the Dance of the Deer Ceremony. As I said, if the hunters were going to take a deer's life, it had to be done in a sacred way or the animal's spirit would not return to the forest—then all the deer would eventually disappear. The Ceremony of Mesingwe included the spirits of *all* the animals.

*The Lenape believed that if they did not perform this ceremony in the proper way, it would upset the whole animal world—then all the animals would eventually disappear.*

The people depended so much on these animals. They believed that all things have their own spirit. I know that gets a little "way out" for modern man. Another way to look at it is all living things have energy, or life force. I'm trying to find a beginning of why modern man broke from that understanding. Perhaps it's because the Bible says that man was created in God's image. That separated man from Nature?

After the ceremonies, and then the feast, the families and bands dispersed into the forest to their winter camps and villages.

### Thanksgiving Ceremonies: Late Fall

In the late fall, the Iroquois, the Narragansett, and other northern and New England tribes had a Thanksgiving Ceremony. This usually took place at the end of the harvest. The time depended on a tribe's geographical location and weather. I think the Iroquois people still have these Thanksgiving ceremonies intact in a bigger way than the other eastern tribes.

*Because of their reservation life, some Indians were able to hold on to a lot of their traditions.* In many locations, the reservations are isolated. The people didn't have a lot of outside influence to prevent them from performing their ceremonies. The isolation of reservation life has had that one good effect, but overall—life there was and is very bad.

Some Indians who have stepped into the dominant society look at these ceremonies as backwards because they lost the connection to their culture.

**The Season of the Clacking Stones: Early Winter**

The Season of the Clacking Stones came right after the Thanksgiving ceremonies. As winter set in, the people spent more time inside their wigwams. They made sure they kept their activities interesting and engaging. There were many functions and activities that kept the young ones physically and mentally active.

Winter was a time to teach the children how to make all the various tools and crafts. Stones were used to make hatchets and corn grinders. The name of the season comes from the clacking sound when stones are hit together to form a groove in the hatchet stone or to shape the stone into a tool. Because most villages were near waterways, it was said you could hear the sound of the clacking stones in the village from a great distance. Sound travels far along those waterways.

*It was a storytelling time: a time for the elders to teach the children the oral history of the tribe around the campfire.* It was also a time for passing down tribal laws and stories about their leaders and elders.

## Mid-Winter

During mid-winter, it was customary for small groups of people from different villages to walk to other villages to see who was in trouble, who had sickness, who had passed on, or if their food supplies were running low.

The group who made those journeys brought extra food with them. If they came to a village that needed food, they held a big feast. That not only helped the physical needs of the people, but it uplifted them spiritually, knowing that family and friends were concerned. Today, some individuals still carry on this tradition.

## Feast of the Dead

This was a ceremony practiced by our relatives, the Piscataways, in the Chesapeake region. They buried the bones of their dead in communal graves or ossuaries. Immediately after death, the bodies were placed on a scaffold, or buried with a temporary funeral that held them until the final communal burial. The dead were then prepared for that final burial and spirit journey in a ceremony called the Feast of the Dead. It was held when enough people had died to be placed together in a communal ossuary. That way, they would not have to go on their journey alone.

## Ceremonies for Children

With many of the tribes, a ceremony wasn't given to a child until they were about two years old. Those first two years were kind of iffy—they didn't feel that the child actually belonged to them until after that. I guess there was a lot of mortality before that time. From two years on, we had ceremonies recognizing different achievements of the children. They may have ventured out on their own to learn a particular skill, such as imitating various bird and animal sounds, animal tracking, hunting, fishing, or learning how to fit into their natural surroundings. Maybe a child had taken an interest in aspects of village life or conquered certain fears. Those children then were given a ceremony to encourage them to continue on their path and realize that the tribe was proud of their achievements.

## The Name-Giving Ceremony

The Name-Giving Ceremony is probably one of the oldest ceremonies on this continent. This ceremony varies from tribe to tribe and group to group. The Name-Giving is considered sacred because the name is a connection to the Great Spirit, or Creator. To associate that person with the Creator, the name referred to something in Nature. When people see names like Charging Buffalo or Running Deer, they think these names are powerful and represent something strong, but that's not the way it is in Nature. *In Nature, all things are powerful.* The Creator gave everything its own power. Look at the field mouse; his power is to see things up close, in detail. Opalaniye, the Eagle, flies high—his power is to see across far distances.

Today, some Indians select their own names. That's not how it was done in the past. Traditionally, a relative or someone close to a child selected his or her name. The name had a special significance. In the past, children were given their names around the age of four. Prior to that, a child was referred to as the son or daughter of say, Running Deer.

In preparation for the Name-Giving Ceremony there is fasting, then the Sweat Lodge Ceremony. The sweat cleanses the body and heart. The Sweat Lodge Ceremony represents returning to the womb of Mother Earth. At age four, there is a certain amount of fear of the sweat lodge, and overcoming that fear is, in a sense, a step toward becoming an adult.

After they come out of the sweat lodge and go through the Name-Giving Ceremony, it is as if they were reborn. There is a closing prayer and a feast afterwards. With most tribes, the child's name stayed with them the rest of their lives.

Today, some Indian people name their child early in life, before the Name-Giving Ceremony. Let's say a father had an experience with a particular animal and wanted that to be a part of his child's life; he would use that animal in the child's name. It was usually something spiritual.

An adult will go through the Name-Giving Ceremony to receive his or her Indian name for the first time. If you are an Indian, an English name takes your Indian identity away from you. *If you have an Indian name that refers to the Natural World, your name will have more meaning and power.*

Maybe you saw something in a vision that came to you that suggested a name. Or, someone may give you a new name based on a personal characteristic or something special that took place in your life.

The first Name-Giving I was ever involved with came to me through Chief Billy Red Wing Tayac and his son Mark, both Piscataway Indians. It took place at the Grove in Salem County, New Jersey. The Grove is a wooded area owned by one of our council women where we camped and had our ceremonies. It was a Name-Giving Ceremony for Lewis Pierce, a council member of the Nanticoke Lenni-Lenape Tribe. It was organized by Chief Red Wing. First, Lew went through the purification consisting of a one-day fast and the Sweat Lodge Ceremony. The people involved were smudged with the smoke from the red cedar (for purification) before they entered the circle. In the center of the circle was a fire. Chief Red Wing's son, Mark Tayac, gave the opening prayer, a high-pitched chant facing the four directions. The prayer was very powerful.

Chief Red Wing, who was close to Lew, had selected Graysquirrel to be Lew's Indian name. The gray squirrel is known as an animal that is always taking care of business, making sure its family is secure. Lew was really on the ball and took care of his family in everything that he did, so he became Graysquirrel. Right after the name was given, Graysquirrel took that moment for a prayer, and as an offering, dropped some red cedar into the fire. The smoke of the cedar symbolically carries our prayers up to the Creator. Three of Lew's friends made a pledge to always be there whenever he needed help. If he called, they were to come to his aid. Open prayers were then given around the sacred circle. My open prayer was giving thanks for my grandmother and her influence on me. Then there was a closing prayer followed by a feast. Afterward, Graysquirrel's family presented gifts to all of those present.

The most recent Name-Giving Ceremony I attended was in Cheswold, Delaware. Chief Dennis White Otter Coker, organized the ceremony and led the purification (smudging) of the attendees as they entered the circle. There was an opening prayer, and Chief White Otter asked me to speak. I spoke about the Name-Giving Ceremony being one of the oldest of ceremonies known to this land.

I said, "The Name-Giving Ceremony is very sacred and serious, and I hope that everyone participating understands that."

There were several people in the circle who were receiving their new Indian names. Chief White Otter asked who was receiving their name. That person was asked to come up and joined him in the center of the circle by the fire. The person giving the name was also asked to join them. Chief White Otter then asked that person to reveal the name to him and he announced that name to everyone. The person giving the name may explain to the chief what that name means and why it was selected. The chief then would convey that to those in the circle.

One woman gave her grandmother the name Patient Turtle. She explained that she gave her that name because of her grandmother's patience and understanding. Her grandmother was a quiet person. Knowing her, you knew she always had your best interests at heart; she was always there for you. Chief White Otter then walked Patient Turtle around the circle in a clockwise direction. He stopped at each of the four directions and called out her new name four times.

He announced that, "From this day forward, she will be known as Patient Turtle." After that, she said a prayer and then dropped some red cedar into the fire. Likewise, everyone in the circle who received their new names paused individually to speak, or had a moment of silent prayer, and dropped their red cedar offering into the fire. Then, there was a closing prayer, and afterwards, a feast.

In the past, Lenape girls and boys were usually considered adults by age 14. By then, they had been exposed to their responsibilities all through those early years, so when they turned 14 they were prepared to be adults. That's when they were sent on a Vision Quest—a transition into full adulthood. Afterwards, they received a spiritual name from an elder based on their individual Vision Quest experiences. Generally, that name became their tribal name used within the tribe and village. Sometimes this spiritual name would be revealed to only a few people or just within their family. This was usually a decision by a medicine person and thc parents.

Today, Indian people are coming in contact with each other more than they have in over a hundred years. Here in the East, most of the Lenape ceremonies have been lost, and very few people practice them. Some are still practiced by the Lenape in Oklahoma and up at the Six Nations Reservation in Brantford, Ontario, in Canada.

Urie Fox Sparrow Ridgeway is a member of the Nanticoke Lenni-Lenape Tribe in New Jersey. He is introducing many of the Lenape ceremonies that have been lost. He spent time with the Lenape people in Oklahoma, Brantford, and other tribes. Some tribes have adopted ceremonies, powwows, and spiritual gatherings from Indians of the western reservations because a lot of their traditions are still intact.

Today, many of the Indian people in Delaware and New Jersey practice the Christian faith. So when it comes to weddings, baptisms, and things like that, they usually follow whatever church they belong to. Traditionally, our ceremonies were tribal events and were tied in to what was paramount at a particular season. During the rest of the seasons, the Lenape people were either on the move or spending more time outside harvesting.

# 6.
# A SPIRITUAL WAY OF LIFE

*"When I pass on and return to Mother Earth, my spirit will be a part of all Creation. I will be here in the wind, the rain, the snow, the mountains, the creeks, and the forests." -Chief Quiet Thunder*

## The Sacred Earth

The Earth is sacred to the traditional people of all tribes. It might be celebrated in different ways, but that is the universal theme. All of Creation is considered sacred. For those who still seek traditional ways, Mother Earth is the giver of all life and the final resting place. In our religion, we come from Mother Earth and we go back to Mother Earth only to return again, maybe not in the same form, but as part of the never-ending cycle of life.

*We call our spiritual journey the Good Red Path, living a connection to the Creator and realizing that we are a part of the Creation. With that comes a sacred obligation to protect Turtle Island.*

## Our Tribal Religion

Our original religion was one the people believed in because it helped us stay in balance with each other and the Earth. To my ancestors, everything in the Natural World made sense.

*Created by God, Nature is the giver and the sustainer of all life: it's real, it's good, and enables us all to exist. We looked at life through the eyes of Nature in its natural state. In our observation of Nature, we learned about the Creator and based our religion on the Creation. We pray to Creation because we know it is a manifestation of God the Creator.*

It is not a coincidence that the entrance to our wigwams, tipis, wickiups, and igloos opened to the East. That was in North America, Canada, South America, and Central America. Each morning when we stepped from those dwellings, the first thing we saw was the sun. That was to remind us to pray and thank the Creator for all the gifts that have been given to us. The people were early risers. Seeing the sun rise was important, and by praying as the sun rose, we were acknowledging the Creator. When the Europeans saw Indian people praying as the sun rose, they thought we were praying to the sun as our god—that's not exactly true.

*The Creator manifests power in that huge ball of fire with light, warmth, and the promise of a new day. We could see the Creator in the Sun, but we could also see the Creator in the Wind, the Rain, the Snow, the Mountains, the Forests, the Oceans, the Animals, and the Birds. And because we are a part of all Creation, we could see the Creator in ourselves.*

That morning prayer was to thank the Creator for bringing us through the night, that we are alive, and thankful for another day. Then there are individual things, such as a child might be ill and asking for the Creator to help, maybe to find certain plants that can help heal the child. If there was an important decision to make, we might pray to the Creator for guidance. Mainly, it was giving thanks for all the blessings that we had. That takes in more than I could ever understand. I'm sure that with the simplicity of their world, there were so many things to thank the Creator for—that the fish still migrate upstream in the spring, that the people had enough food stored for the winter, or their child was born without any serious problems—things of that nature.

Not long after I moved to Delaware, word got around about my cultural programs, and Delores Sapieriza, the Head of Continuing Education at Delaware State University, asked me to do a program there. Mostly faculty attended the first program: professors and teachers at the college. During the break, one lady came over and asked a question.

She said, "Did the Lenape have any ceremonies dealing with rain?" I told her they did but I didn't know much about them, only that the weasel was a part of them. She pressed on and asked, "Well, what about rain dances?"

I said, "Do you mean like with some of the southwestern Indians?"

"Yes."

I said, "Well, you know, that's their way."

She said, "You don't really believe that do you?" I could tell by the way she said it, more was coming.

So I said, "Can I ask you a personal question?"

"Yes."

I asked if she practiced any religion. She said, "I am a practicing Roman Catholic."

I said, "Can I ask you another question? Do you believe in the power of prayer?"

Looking at me, she cocked her head to the side and said, "Why, certainly!"

I said, "Well, those ceremonies the southwestern Indians perform are not frivolous. The Rain Dance is a powerful prayer combining the ceremony, the chants, and the dancing. They're not asking for tonight's lottery number or a new Cadillac. They pray for rain. If they don't get rain on their crops, they stand to be in a very serious situation: the possibility of starving to death." Then it was time to start the second half of the program.

Later, when I was packing up, she came up to me and said, "You know Dick, I never thought of it that way."

Today, we have gotten so far away from Nature that many feel superior to it. How can you be superior to something that without it you don't exist? In our religion, for all the things that we enjoyed in Nature, we give our bodies back to Mother Earth and fertilize the land. Plants are nourished from our fertilization, and animals feed on those plants, and life continues on.

My Medicine Bag consists of soil from the burial grounds of my ancestors. As I explain to people, *"It's not just soil; it's the blood and the flesh and the bones of my ancestors who have gone back to Mother Earth to continue the natural cycle of life."*

This land, Turtle Island, consists of thousands of years of Indian people returning to the Mother Earth.

## The Original Instructions

*The Creator placed Indian people in this land and gave us all the gifts and resources of the land and a sacred obligation to protect them.*

Many people who I've come in contact with over the years didn't think the Lenape Indians had religious beliefs because we didn't have a written language. But our most ancient religious laws are the Original Instructions. These were given to our ancestors by the Creator of all life. The elders passed those instructions on to the new generations through the spoken word. *The Lenape followed those instructions as a sacred obligation: that was what kept us in harmony with Nature*. Let me illustrate this with a story.

Years ago, Professor Harry Gershenowitz at Glassboro State College (now Rowan University) had me present a program for his students. I opened up with a question: "Why do some birds fly south in the winter and return north in the spring?"

Professor Gershenowitz stood up and said, "That's very simple, Dick, that's instinct."

I said, "Well, that's a fancy word to explain something." Then I said, "Why do some plants and some insects go to sleep in the winter and reawaken in the spring? Why do some fish, hatched in freshwater streams in a gravel bed, swim out to the ocean in saltwater to mature as adults, then return back to that same stream many years later to reproduce and drop their eggs over the same gravel bed (providing man has not dammed up the streams)? Why does the Sun rise in the East and set in the West? Why does the moon rise in the East and set in the West? Is that also instinct?"

"Traditional Indian people refer to their religious laws as the Original Instructions.

They have the knowledge the Creator passed on to our ancestors through visions and dreams—that *all* of Creation and *all* living things were given these instructions. They could see clearly how the Creation worked, like the fish and birds returning, the rising and setting of the Sun and moon, and all the cycles of Nature. They saw how the animals and all of life tied into the cycle of life—that's how *we* are supposed to tie into it."

*The ancients handed down this knowledge in the form of Original Instructions through stories and legends so it could be comprehended and passed on through the spoken word.*

The word *instinct* doesn't cover it. These instructions represent principles of natural law that keep everything in harmony and balance. All living things follow these Original Instructions except man. Man was given the power to choose. *It is man who is out of balance and is causing an imbalance within Nature.*

You will hear some people say things like, "That guy acts like an animal." Well, that's an insult to the animal because if that animal is left alone and man does not disturb it, that animal will follow those instructions. What would happen if the sun did not rise in the East, but rose in the West? What would happen if the moon reversed? All these things are designed in a way that man will never understand—it is beyond his capability. The Creator has designed the Creation in such a way that everything works, and it works in balance. Traditional Indian people followed the Original Instructions given to man:

*Never take more than you need from Nature. Never feel that you are superior to Nature. Always respect Nature, and learn to live within the Natural Cycles to be as One with Nature.* A Ho Ka!

**The Seventh-Generation Philosophy**

*"I see a time of Seven Generations when all the colors of mankind will gather under the Sacred Tree of Life and the whole Earth will become One Circle again." -Crazy Horse, Oglala Lakota*

*"Truth crushed to Earth shall rise again." -Chief Quiet Thunder*

The Seventh-Generation Philosophy states that for all of Nature's gifts we enjoy today, we have a *sacred obligation* to insure that seven generations of people in the future will have those same gifts—not to live just for today, or live for one's self, but to *live for seven generations in the future. We tried to never take more than was needed, and always put something back in return.* We used everything we harvested, giving thanks to the Creator for all those gifts. *As long as we were in control of the land, we stood by that obligation.* That is what sustained and kept *everything* harmonious. Because of that, there was always a great abundance of resources in the land. There is a legend, not just with the Lenape, but also with many tribes:

> *The Seventh Generation will stand and reclaim their heritage. Truth crushed to Earth shall rise again, and the Seventh Generation bears that truth—of our place in the Creation, and our responsibility to maintain it.*

Traditional Indians are pointing the way by bringing back this ancient understanding. We are the beginning of that generation and there is no end. As far as I can ascertain, I am one of the Seventh Generation and have a responsibility to stand up and speak that truth. I have talked to other Indian people from across this land and they have said the same thing. I believe it, and I think a lot of non-Indian people believe they are also part of it. Since my life started, there has been an avalanche of activity within the Indian world. The Second World War was an opportunity for many Indians to defend this country and other countries overrun by the Germans and Japanese. That gave many of them new life—a chance to become warriors again.

In the 1970s, the American Indian Movement (AIM) protest at Wounded Knee opened the eyes of the country and the world to the injustices placed on Indian people. A majority of the people in North America had forgotten we were here. The reservation Indians were never heard from. The ones surrounded by the dominant society were struggling to

survive, and many had stepped across the line and became part of the dominant society. Many Indians had even forgotten who they were. AIM was influential in bringing back Indian awareness and pride. From that movement, some conditions started to gradually improve. Indians were standing up and speaking out. Tribes started to organize all across the country. My people got organized and we eventually gained State recognition as The Nanticoke Lenni-Lenape Tribal Nation of New Jersey.

Now, Seventh-Generation Indians are on the move and reclaiming their heritage. Today, the new National Museum of the American Indian in Washington, DC is going to change the Indian world as well as the entire world. People will see something they never expected. Instead of viewing Indian people as barbaric savages, they will realize we have a special connection to this land and a deep understanding of Nature. They will see that Indian culture encompasses language, art, religion, music, environmental initiatives, and ceremony—the connections between all peoples, Nature, and the Earth. I anticipate there will be more demand for Indian people to speak and give educational programs like I do in the near future. In recent years, I have found there are non-Indian people who know a lot more about Indian cultures than I do by information I've seen on the internet. Many are making a concerted effort to gather this information. I want people to understand that having traditional values means more than dressing up in a ribbon shirt and dancing at a powwow—you are walking the Good Red Path.

*We want to give people an understanding that in a short 500 years the dominant society has polluted the water, the land, the air, and upset the balance of Nature.*

The critical issue of the past was the land, the critical issue of the present is the land, and the critical issue of the future will be the land. It is all about Mother Earth. As the living conscience of our nation, traditional Indian people have a responsibility to create that awareness. The destruction of our *Living World* will not stop unless we *all* take responsibility for it.

Today, even the smallest thing, such as recycling, can make a difference. People can buy their groceries in reusable shopping bags so they don't have to use plastic bags. We can take actions to conserve trees. We can conserve energy by using LED lights and turning off lights when we leave the room.

*These can all have a big impact. That's what I'm trying to get across.*

**The Sacred Circle**

Symbolism is big with traditional Indian people, and the circle is a sacred symbol to almost all Indian people.

The seal of our tribe is enclosed in a circle. All of the circles and cycles in Creation are considered sacred. The circle has its own power; it has no beginning or end. We begin with the Earth, which is round and has its own power. The sun is round; it also has its own power. The moon is round and has its own power. The stars are round; they have their own powers. The sun, moon, and planets have orbits in balance. The four seasons are circular. The cycles of life are circular, a cycle from infancy to childhood, to adulthood, to old age, and back to Mother Earth. The life force is a power within itself and helps keep all the other circles and cycles balanced. It's the continuance of life—never ending.

*The circle is also a symbol of the Creator and all the power in Creation.* It is continuing energy—being connected to everything that we know to be powerful and part of the Creation.

The circle plays an important role in all of our ceremonies. The drum is round. We form a circle around a central fire and dance in a circle. Before a ceremony, we have an opening prayer, inviting the Creator into the circle. For the Sundance Ceremony, we prepare mentally and physically through the Sweat Lodge Ceremony, the fasting, and the prayers. If we go into that circle, we've made a very serious commitment. I don't know of anyone who has completed the Sundance who didn't truly believe that what they were doing was sacred. Because we are performing in that *sacred circle*, we become connected in a sacred way to all of Creation.

Sometimes, people ask me to dance, and I tell them I don't dance. If it's a young student, I'll take the time to explain why I don't dance in public. I dance during certain seasons. To me, dancing is very sacred and ties into the religion of this land. Whenever I dance, it is usually alone or with very close friends and not always Indian friends. Powwows are both commercial and educational events. Indian people love to dance. Dancing is acceptable for public display if the dance circle has not been blessed for a ceremonial purpose. If the dance circle has been blessed for the purpose of performing a ceremony, it becomes a *sacred circle*: then money and rewards should never be involved.

If performed in a respectful way for cultural and educational reasons, the powwow dancing can promote tribalism in a good way. I find that when the non-Indian sees Indians dancing in regalia and feathers, they often consider it a form of entertainment. Maybe in some cases it is, but my dancing is for a spiritual purpose—it's my connection to the Creator. That's one of the reasons I don't dance at powwows. I tell people that I don't want to be considered an entertainer. I would rather be thought of as an educator. That's part of this connection I still have with Mother Earth. I consider it very sacred.

Today, when too many people are involved, not everyone takes it seriously.

It's like, "Okay, I've got my Indian name now," but not really understanding they're committing themselves to something greater. A non-Indian from the church once asked me if it was all right for him to wear a ribbon shirt.

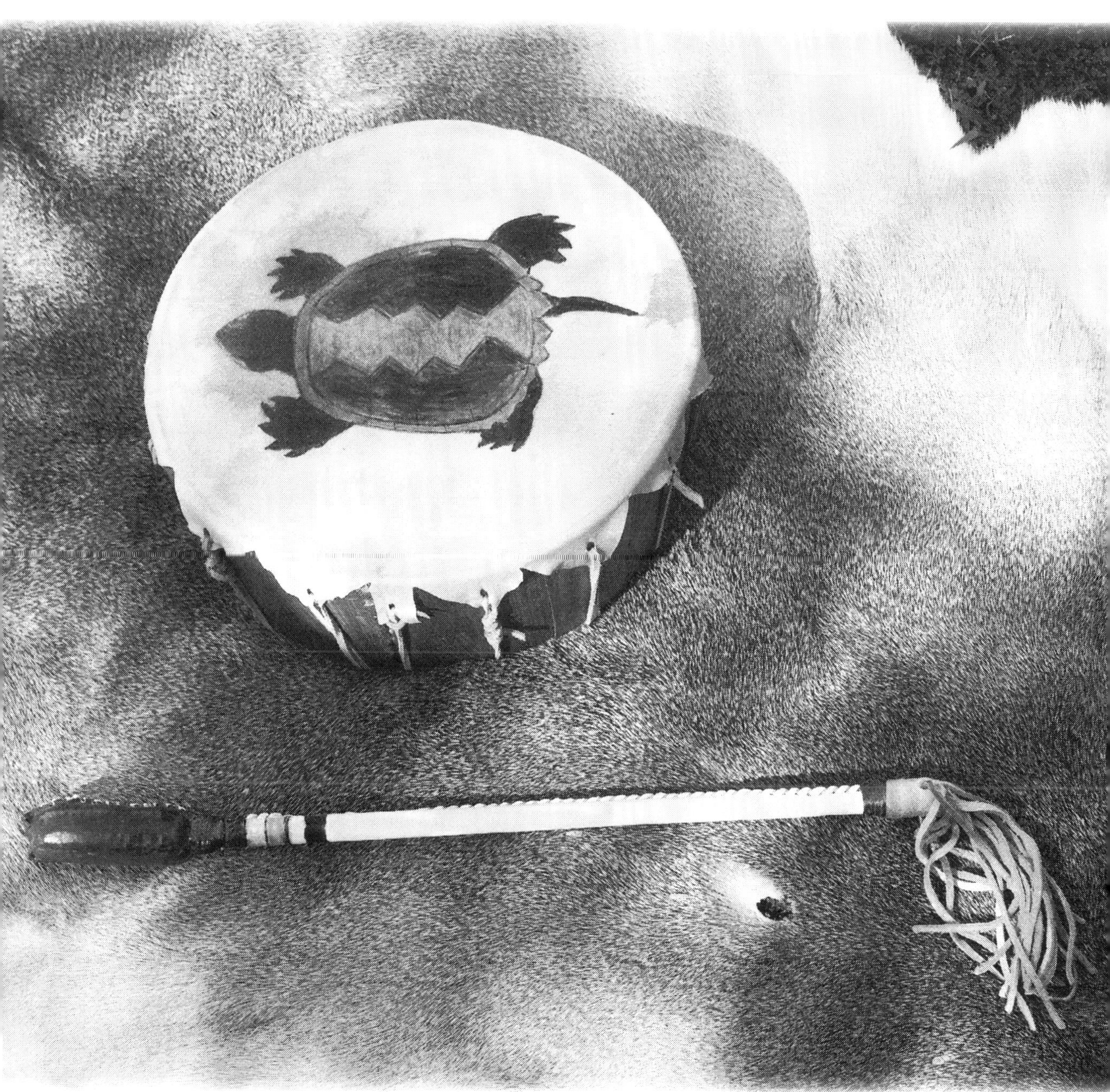

I said, "Why did you ask me that?" He told me that some people he knew (I know them too) told him that he had no right to wear a ribbon shirt.

I said, "Well, you know, there's no great significance to wearing a ribbon shirt. Some non-Indians admire our culture and want to be included in it. Many times the general audience is invited to come and dance."

He then asked me point blank, "What does it mean to be a Native American?"

I said, "It means having a commitment to something that is greater than you. *You are making a commitment to walk that Good Red Path—a connection through Mother Earth to the Creator."*

## The Sweat Lodge

*The Sweat Lodge Ceremony represents going back to the womb of Mother Earth.*

The sweat lodge is used by most of the Indian tribes I am familiar with in many parts of North America. The Sweat Lodge Ceremony was performed before a Vision Quest, before the hunt, and as a part of most of our important spiritual ceremonies. The sweat lodge was set apart from the village; it was constructed in an area east of where other activities took place. The lodge is made from saplings with the bottom ends driven into the ground, bent over, and tied into a dome shape with saplings tied in circles around the dome. This structure is covered with animal hides with one small opening just big enough for a person to crawl through. Inside, in the womb of Mother Earth, is a central pit where we place heated rocks. Helpers build a bonfire nearby and heat 12 rocks red hot. They use deer antlers to pass these rocks into the sweat lodge and place them into the pit.

The people enter the lodge in a clockwise direction and sit on the ground. Then the entrance is covered with an animal skin. It is pitch-black inside, except for the glow of those 12 red hot rocks. Cedar is dropped on the rocks, bringing up an aromatic smoke to spiritually purify the air. A prayer is spoken. Water is poured onto those hot rocks, producing steam; this creates an intense heat, which permeates everyone. The steam cleanses the body as well as the heart. I don't know of any tribe that doesn't use the sweat

lodge, not just for the physical, but also for the spiritual part: going back to Mother Earth. It brings about a spiritual awareness of our connection to the Creator.

The sweat lodge is used anytime during the year. Sometimes we feel a need to physically cleanse our bodies. Other times, we may start to weaken spiritually and the Sweat Lodge Ceremony gives us that spiritual energy we need. With most of the tribes I know, it is used for both cleansing and spiritual energy. It's like no other experience you can have, and it will stay with you the rest of your life. It is *very* powerful!

## The Vision Quest

The Vision Quest is a passage into adulthood. It is a quest for understanding and connection to spirit.

You will find that we speak more about the men, but women also do the Vision Quest. Many Indian tribes in North America have practiced the Vision Quest since ancient times, though it's not always done the same way. Generally, when a young person reached the age of 11 to 14 years, life started to get a little serious. They are approaching manhood or womanhood, and at that stage in life they're not that sure of themselves.

There are many reasons why a person goes on a Vision Quest. In my understanding, it's to reach out to the Creator and ask for help when seeking your path in life. One may seek a spiritual guide that could come in the form of an animal, bird, or plant, such as the Eagle or the Cedar Tree. These guides all have significant meanings. Each guide has certain attributes, such as the wisdom of the Owl for someone seeking wisdom. Seekers may take a Vision Quest to solve a specific problem. In the process, they are reaching out to the Creator. They are seeking a spiritual connection that will anchor them so they can have a fulfilled life as a good tribal brother or sister, or a good citizen, as we say today.

Seekers may go through a Sweat Lodge Ceremony first to purify their mind, body, and spirit. Sometimes, before their Vision Quest they will perform a Pipe Ceremony. With the Medicine Pipe, they are acknowledging the Creator. It slows things down so they can think clearly about what's about to take place and their reasons for taking the quest. It opens the door to spiritual understanding.

The seekers go alone to a preselected, isolated area where they will remain in silent vigil. They need isolation to disconnect from people and everyday thoughts. They are usually confined within a ten-foot diameter quest circle. The size of the circle may vary with the tribe. During the Vision Quest, they fast for four days and four nights and seek a dream or a vision. The idea is to stay in one spot and pray for a vision. Isolation is necessary to remove all distractions from what they are seeking. Sometimes the vision will come in less than four days. It could take more. If they are fortunate to receive that vision and understand their path in life; it brings them peace and harmony within. Certain things may be also be revealed such as personal gifts or special qualities they aren't aware of. If they were blessed to have that vision come, whatever it was, that was factored into their new spiritual name.

With many tribes, when the seekers returned from their Vision Quest uncertain about the meaning of their vision, they would seek the help of a medicine person. A medicine person can interpret that experience and give them a spiritual name referring to that vision. The medicine person can also interpret the circumstances in their vision or dream and how it ties into their life. The medicine person was usually from their tribe and knew the seeker's background.

This is still the way many Western Plains Indians get their spiritual names. Usually, only a few people know their spiritual name. Today, there are many distractions that block us from reaching out to the Creator and the Spirit World. The Vision Quest is vital today not just for traditional Indians, but for anyone who is trying to find their way.

*I believe the Vision Quest is needed more now than in the past 500 years.*

**Medicine Power**

*Medicine is considered to be anything that connects us with Nature or with the Creator.*

We believe the Eagle has this special connection with the Creator. The Eagle is the bird that flies the highest and symbolizes that connection between the Creator and Indian people. We symbolically send our prayers up to the Creator by the Eagle. I believe most tribes consider the Eagle a very sacred bird because of this Medicine Power. That is why Eagle feathers and fans are so important for the practice of our native religions. If we are sending a prayer to the Creator in a Sweat Lodge Ceremony, or in any other ceremony, the Eagle feather fan assures that our prayers are conducted in the proper way.

Medicine also applies to people relative to each other. Tom Brown Jr. (The Tracker) has a saying when you are departing: "All Good Medicine," meaning all good spirits, all good things. I guess it's like when some people say, "May God be with you," or something to that respect.

One of our medicine items the dominant culture has adopted and exploited for commercial gain is the Dreamcatcher. I've been told that the Ojibwa (or Chippewa) people first came up with the idea of hanging one in the area where a child sleeps. When the bad dreams come, they get caught in the webbing because they don't know there is a little hole in the center. The good dream knows how to find that center hole and comes through. So the child only gets the good dreams. In the morning, the mother takes the Dreamcatcher outside and exposes it to the sun. The sunlight destroys the bad dreams. I believe all dreams, good or bad, serve a purpose.

**Medicine People**

*Medicine people are very special.*

Let me elaborate because history books didn't do justice in describing our medicine people. Their journey, we believe, comes directly from the Creator. A medicine person is someone who has a vast knowledge of plants and has a function similar to a doctor, but more as a healer. Some healers know medicinal plants and are expert at preparing important herbal medicines. They also conduct healing ceremonies. Often the medicine person was a woman because women have special powers for knowing the different medicines and healing plants. Much of that knowledge comes to them in visions, then there are other ways such as training, testing, and observation.

Medicine people have special abilities in different areas. There were medicine people who would mentally prepare a young person for the sweat lodge and conduct the Sweat Lodge Ceremony. There were medicine people who took a young person under their wing if they saw something special in that person. They groomed him or her to learn the ways and functions of a medicine person. Some medicine people have spiritual power to interpret dreams or see into the future. They are exceptional. For many of these medicine people, their path came about because a sign appeared in a vision directing them to be a healer. Being a medicine person is a heavy responsibility. Their ceremonies must be conducted precisely to be beneficial.

People sometimes ask me how the Indian people knew what plants to take for medicine or what plants were edible. For those who have special powers, their visions and dreams tell them which plants are edible and which medicines are used for certain conditions. That's one reason I think all dreams have a purpose.

*In the old days, Indian people were able to relate to the Natural World without the mental interference we have in today's world. Before European contact, their lives were totally connected to the Natural World, so their dreams were entirely based on that world. They were in that connection and truth day and night.*

Medicine people also gained knowledge from the animals. Sometimes they observed what medicinal plants an animal or bird ate. A communication from an animal spirit may have come to them in response to their prayers for guidance on a healing. They received this guidance through dreams or visions. In many cases, the medicine people believed that the animal was teaching them.

*Back then, within the purity of Nature, dreams and visions had clear and significant meanings. It was an immediate communication; there were no special texts and no monetary payment.*

Now, here in the East, a word to the wise: if someone tells you he or she is a medicine person, erase it from your thoughts. A medicine person has exceptional powers, and there are people who want to flock to the medicine man or woman. A true medicine person will not tell you that they are a medicine person. That information comes from other people who have seen or experienced it or talked to other people who know that person has medicine power. People may say that person has been given certain powers from the Creator.

These powers are to be used to help the people. A Ho Ka!

## Tobacco and the Medicine Pipe

Tobacco is a sacred plant that we used in almost all of our ceremonies and offerings. Tobacco is a gift from the Creator. It originally only grew in this hemisphere. As far as I know, all Eastern Woodland Indians used tobacco in various ways. Tobacco can be made into a powerful medicine. If tobacco was not administered to me, I probably wouldn't be here today because in my first nine winters I almost died from pneumonia.

If we took a life while hunting or gathering plants, we always used tobacco as an offering. It helps clear the air and lets the spirit of that animal or plant know that we are grateful and accountable for taking its life.

In the past, anytime we took part in something as important as a treaty or a ceremony, tobacco was smoked. *When we smoked the Medicine Pipe, the smoke symbolically carried our prayers up to the Creator.*

When someone smoked the Medicine Pipe with another person, it was powerful enough to cease all hostilities between them. When we smoked the Medicine Pipe together, it made us like brothers. So tobacco is a very special, sacred plant. Today, because of all the chemicals added, tobacco is a poison, whereas in the old days it was beneficial.

In 2010, I did a program for the Nanticoke people in lower Delaware at their museum. I talked about the Medicine Pipe and its significance. I talked about how important the Medicine Pipe was and still is.

There is a lot of symbolism involved with the Medicine Pipe. The bowl represents Mother Earth and the female principle. The stem is from the plant world and represents the male principle. The leather fringe is from the animal world, the feathers from the bird world, and the fire from the spirit world. Ceremonial tobacco is a mixture of tobacco and various herbs, depending on the purpose of the ceremony. This tobacco mix represents all things combined into the oneness of life.

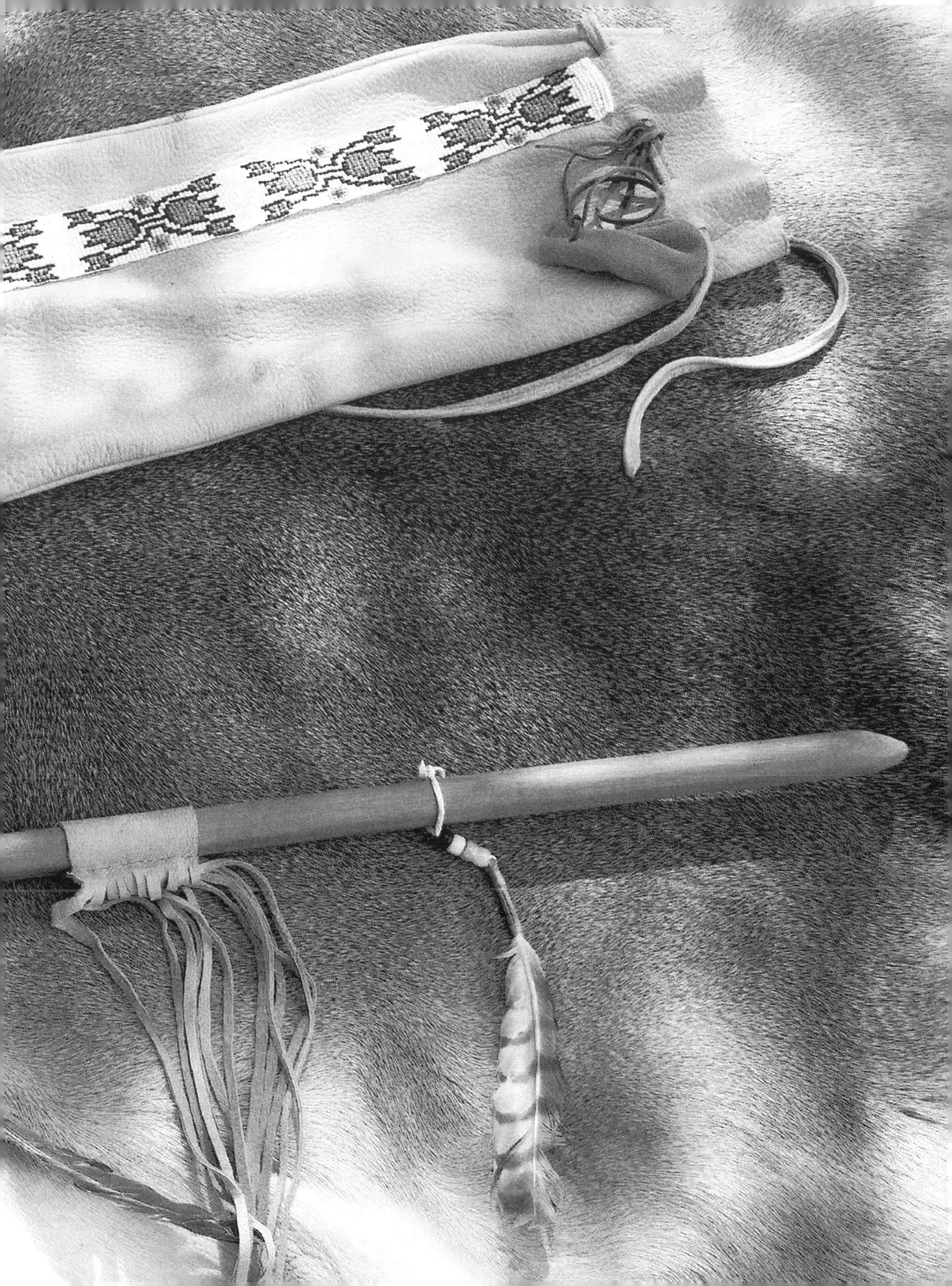

*The Medicine Pipe and the tobacco mixture symbolize truth.* I explained that if you are a Christian and are asked to put your hand on the Bible and swear that everything you say is the truth and nothing but the truth so help you God—if you're a believer, you would tell the truth. It is the same when traditional Indians smoke the Medicine Pipe. We do not inhale the smoke, we exhale it. The smoke mixed with our breath symbolically rises up to the Creator carrying our prayers and promises. Our prayers are combined with the prayers of all living things. Our power comes from the Natural World. When the traditional Indian smokes the Medicine Pipe out in the open and makes an agreement with other people, the Indian believes that all of Creation is a witness.

*As the Bible represents truth for Christians, the Medicine Pipe has that same status with traditional Indians.*

Now, whenever I have a non-Indian audience, I bring up the equation of the Medicine Pipe and the Bible because I think it is valid. To me, it makes a point and brings our religion into focus. It's all part of the Seventh Generation and to make the dominant society aware that we may have been different, but different doesn't mean we were not intelligent. At the peace treaties, the Indians smoked the Medicine Pipe, then passed it to the Europeans.

*Those treaties took place under the Sky, the Clouds, the Wind, the Trees, among the Birds, and Animals.*

After making an agreement with those Europeans, smoking the Medicine Pipe, and exhaling that smoke, they dared not break that agreement because they would be breaking their covenant with the Creator, the Creation, and all of Life. When the Europeans broke those treaties, it was hard for the Indians to understand what kind of people they were. How could they break a covenant they made before the Creation and the Creator? Even today, non-Indians might see Indian people smoke the Medicine Pipe before an event and think it's some form of relaxation or recreation. That is *not* what this is all about. Because many Europeans did not believe we had a functioning and legitimate religion, they never understood that the Medicine Pipe symbolizes truth. A Ho Ka!

## We Are This Land

*"The Earth does not belong to man. Man belongs to the Earth."*
*-Chief Seattle, Suquamish*

Our bodies are what the North American continent is composed of. When our bodies go back to the land—materially and spiritually we become part of the land.

The spirits of our ancestors are still here. The Creator put Indian people in this land, and with that came the *sacred obligation* to protect it. For Indian people, our culture and traditions determines who we truly are. If our traditions are lost, then we are no longer Indian people; we are just like everyone else.

In the early 1980s, when our tribe was trying to obtain some land from Fairfield Township in New Jersey, the tribal council asked me if I would go to the townships where the bulk of our people lived and see if they would donate a portion of the land to us. I was reluctant at first because it meant that I had to start dealing with non-Indian people about a subject that was unheard of—an Indian asking for free land. But I felt good about trying to obtain land for our tribe.

So I went around to the townships, and some non-Indian people were receptive to the idea; it made sense to them. I felt it was the right thing to do and the right time to do it. It's tied-in to the Seventh Generation standing up, speaking out, and reclaiming our heritage. I spoke from the Indians' perspective—what the land meant to us, not regarding its commercial value, but explaining that an Indian is never really whole unless he has a land base where he can go and pray, and hopefully, in time, have burial areas that will never be disturbed.

*I explained that we needed a place where we could go back to our culture and once again become a part of the land.*

I ended my talks with my Medicine Bag. It contains soil from the burial ground of my ancestors. I like to narrate this in the way that I do it.

"In Fairfield Township, in Cumberland County, there is an area where my mother's people have gone for thousands of years to gather medicines and perform ceremonies.

Near that location is where many of my ancestors are buried. *The soil from my Medicine Bag is not just ordinary soil: it consists of the blood, the flesh, and the bones of thousands of years of my ancestors who have died and gone back to Mother Earth to continue the natural cycle.* That's what ties our spirits and souls to this land."

That's why I always told my tribe, *"Seek to have a personal relationship with the Earth—that's what makes us who we are."* That, I believe, separates a traditional Indian from just someone with Indian blood. The traditional Indian either has made that connection to the Earth, or seeks that connection. If you don't have or seek a personal relationship with Mother Earth, then you are losing out on who you really are.

Anyone who is born here is a Native American, but we supersede and go far beyond that. We are *of* the land and *are* the land. We are not just Native Americans; *we are the indigenous people of this land.* My strength comes from my past. The strength that my grandparents and their grandparents had instills in me who I am; that all goes back to our connection to the land. *We are this land!*

## The Eagle Has Returned

About a week after I spoke at the township meetings, I got a call from Cindy Zirkle. She identified herself as an organizer for the Cohansey Area Restoration Project (CARP). She said she recently heard me speak at the Nanticoke Lenni-Lenape Powwow at Bridgeton High School. She asked if I would get involved with her group to try to prevent a commercial development. We laugh about it today because we have become very good friends, but I remember telling her, "Lady, I don't get involved with non-Indians." But she was persistent, and over a period of time she persuaded me to come down and listen to what was involved.

I went down, I listened, and I was impressed. The Cohansey River is the most dominant feature of Nature in Cumberland County. This river is right in the heart of where my mother's people lived. There is a lot of history along that river, which goes back to my tribe. A high bluff overlooks the Cohansey. Along that stretch was the area my mother's people did their fishing, crabbing, and hunting. I got involved when I found out what was going to happen to the Cohansey River. It was in jeopardy of being totally destroyed. Genstar Stone Products, a multinational corporation, wanted to build a large sand-mining operation along with a barge port in Bridgeton. I heard about the huge barges they were going to use to haul sand up and down the Cohansey. The Cohansey River is serpentine—it's designed that way by the Creator to slow the water down so it won't erode the land. Well, those barges were so long, they would have to chop off the river's curves and turns. That would make the water rush down, and then the land would go. The Army Corps of Engineers was going to dredge the river so it would be deep enough for the barges. When I realized what was involved, I thought: well, it's time for me to either put up or shut up. That's what helped me to rise above my resistance to dealing with non-Indians. So I applied myself. My function was to go to the different townships around the Cohansey River and talk about the river from an Indian perspective. I was unsure about what I could do, but I wanted to contribute something to saving the river.

I remember the first night when I went over to the old colonial town of Greenwich. At that meeting, one guy got up right away and said, "This isn't our problem, this is Bridgeton's problem. It's on the other side of the Cohansey." Now, I was not a speaker by any sense of the word. I could talk Indian talk, but I hadn't dealt with non-Indians in this kind of a circumstance. I thought to myself: Boy, how are you going to deal with this?

So I said, "Can I ask you a question?"

"Yes," he said.

I said, "What is your occupation?"

"I am a farmer and I run a clam boat in the summertime. I also do commercial crabbing."

I said, "Well, your Army Corps of Engineers is going to start dredging the Cohansey River in April." I told him about all the toxic poisons that were in that mud. "Once they start dredging, those poisons are going to come up and move down the river and into the bay. So those clams are going to start dying." I mean this was some powerful stuff that had been accumulating in that mud for years.

"It's not just a Bridgeton problem. It's a problem for anybody who lives along this river, and by you being a clammer—it's going to affect you." Well, that kind of changed things, and it gave me more backbone—I realized I could deal with these situations. As I learned more about this project, I found out about the politics involving high officials. Even worse than that, a whole area in Bridgeton called Southeast Avenue (where the depot would be built) is a blighted area. It's been designated a blighted area since the 1950s, meaning that it could be condemned any time. Mostly poor Black people lived there. If this went through, Southeast Avenue was going to be condemned—not just one street, but whole neighborhoods. Where would those people go? So we were trying to come up with ideas to try to slow this project down. The people fighting it were just those living along the Cohansey River.

We didn't have money, but we did have a young environmental lawyer from Trenton who took our case. He only charged for his expenses because we couldn't pay him for his actual work. We finally raised enough money to conduct our own environmental impact study. In that mud we found arsenic, strychnine, PCBs, DDT, and other things that I'd never heard of, which came from agriculture and manufacturing over the years. It all went into the streams and wound up in the Cohansey River mud. The timing couldn't have been worse. The Army Corps of Engineers was planning to dredge right when the herring would be migrating up the river to spawn. Dredging would stir up that mud, and those poisons would go down the river, into the herring, into the bay, and into the food chain. It would destroy the river, and the bay, and more.

We were kicking some ideas around, and somebody mentioned that the Bald Eagle was on the endangered species list. Maybe, if we built an Eagle's nest, and we could entice the Eagles to return, that might have an impact. (Most of the Eagles in New Jersey had been decimated by DDT, a pesticide widely used on crops, until Rachael Carson wrote *The Silent Spring* and the poison was banned.) About a year went by, and the Army Corps of Engineers had set a date to start dredging the river in the middle of April. So we came up with an Eagle-nesting project. One of the people had property by the river bordering a cove where we planned to build the nest. A big snowstorm started Thursday night and lasted all day Friday.

On Saturday morning, everything was covered in snow, and it was calm. As we walked east to the nest site, the sun came up through the trees like a huge orange ball—one of the most beautiful things I have ever seen. I realized this was a very special morning. We were fortunate to have the assistance of Larry Niles from the New Jersey Fish and Game Commission. He was involved with bringing the Eagles from Manitoba, Canada, into New Jersey. He and his brother did the climbing, and the rest of us gathered the material. It was quite a sight. We started with chicken wire, and then we hoisted tree limbs up, and gradually the limbs got smaller and smaller. We worked all morning, then stopped and had our lunch in the woods. We worked again all afternoon.

When the nest was finished, a huge man couldn't stretch his arms from one side to the other. That's how big it was, and it was sturdy. It was beside a quiet cove, so it was an ideal spot for Eagles to fish. If I were an Eagle, I would move right in! I could just visualize the Eagles there. After the nest was finished, the people asked if I would do something spiritual. I performed a Pipe Ceremony and spoke a prayer asking for the Eagle to come back to the land—to return to the river.

This was my prayer:

*Oh Great Spirit,*

*We come here today in the open, Indian and non-Indian alike.*

*We come hoping that you will bless what we are trying to do.*

*We have abused this gift, our Mother Earth.*

*We come today to bring the Eagles back to the river*

*where echoes of their songs will be heard once more*

*up and down this river.*

*Great Spirit, we ask your blessing.*

*May you smile upon this, which we try to do.*

*Bring the Eagle, Opalaniye, the gift: the bird that flies high.*

*May we send our prayers once more upon the wings of Opalaniye*

*up to you, The Creator: The Creator of All Life.*

*Today we try once more to live in balance, to follow your*

*Original Instructions.*

*May we be worthy of all these gifts and blessings you have given us.*

*Bring the mighty Eagle back to the river.*

*A Ho Ka!*

After the prayer, I placed a tobacco offering around the base of the tree.

A year went by, and things were going badly for us. It looked as though we were going to lose. On a Monday afternoon, the two judges who were supposed to make the final decision on this project took a boat trip on the Cohansey River from the bay all the way to Bridgeton. When they got to Bridgeton where the port was to be built, there was an Eagle sitting in a tree. After the judges saw that Eagle, things started going our way. Finally, the decision was made to stop the Genstar development. Today, many Eagles nest along the Cohansey River and the other rivers around it.

That summer, we had a big party down on the Cohansey River where Cindy Zirkle lives. They were talking about the Genstar development and all the effort that went into fighting it, you know—this one and that one did such and such. When they got down to me, Cindy said, "Dick, I know this would never have happened if it hadn't have been for your spiritual involvement." That was the first time anyone other than family members had said anything like that to me. I have talked to my tribe over the years, and I've tried to get them to understand that they have a very special relationship with this land. I know some members of my tribe thought I was backwards in my thinking, but we stopped the Cohansey project, and it was big money. It involved a multi-billion dollar outfit from England.

For the first time, I found out you *can* fight city hall and win. You are probably going to get bloodied up a bit, and even though you are up against a stacked deck, you *can* win if your cause is right. It encouraged me. It has gone even farther than that. Now there are Eagles all around Cumberland and Salem counties, and I like to think I had something to do with that.

During the time I was involved with CARP, some of my tribal members turned their backs on me. They said, "Can't you see these people are using you to protect their properties?"

I said, "I have talked to you about your obligation to protect Mother Earth. Now, I have to put up or shut up. I have to do my bit." I had been on the original tribal council for 13 years and was instrumental in getting our State recognition. I was pretty well respected, and to have my tribal brothers and sisters turn their backs on me—it hurt. I rose above the racial situation even at the cost of losing the respect of tribal members.

With that Eagle project, I knew I did the right thing. It gave me a reason to work with non-Indians and to look at the broader picture. It was about the land and the river. It was a time for me to act on what I had been talking about: that *sacred obligation. It was a real turning point in my life, setting me in my current direction as an educator.*

For years, I never said anything about what happened to anyone other than to my family and my brother, Jim Three Buck, who had encouraged me. Together, we performed ceremonies and prayers along the river thanking the Creator for giving us the opportunity to walk in the lands of our ancestors.

A few years back, Jean Jones, a reporter who was aware of the CARP project, asked me to come to the Eagles' nest and tell her what had taken place. I pretty much told her what I told you, pointing out the nest. That made front-page headlines in the local paper. It was the first time my tribal brothers and sisters realized that Quiet Thunder had something to do with the Eagles they were now seeing. I have noticed that many of the ones who turned their backs on me now have a different attitude.

# 7.
# IT'S THEIR WORLD WE ARE LEAVING THEM

*"We do not inherit the Earth from our ancestors—we borrow it from our Children."*
*-Chief Seattle, Suquamish*

**Teaching as a Career**

By the early 1980s, my tribe had organized, and we were rolling along pretty good. We were receiving grants from the government, and some of those grants stipulated that we had to go into the school systems and do cultural programs. At the same time, when we got established on the powwow circuit, I did my program about the Lenape Indians. This was the first time I was exposed to the general population as a presenter. People were listening to me and some became very interested. Then, the tribal center starting getting calls from teachers asking me to do school programs for them.

Christine Wilson, a teacher, had seen an article in the local paper about me. She brought me into her fourth-grade class to do a cultural program. It was at the Elwood Kindle School in Pitman, New Jersey. Then, she had me come back every year. When I first started doing these programs, the school history books had virtually nothing about the Lenape Indians. A few schools only had something about the western Indians. Around that time, I was starting to get asked to do programs in different schools. They said I really brought the Indian spirit to my programs. Christine Wilson told me the teachers wanted to petition the New Jersey State Board of Education to put Lenape history in their curriculum because it was missing, and the Lenape Indians were so much a part of the history of New Jersey.

She said, "Quiet Thunder was definitely the inspiration for us to put the Lenape Indians into our fourth-grade curriculum. I don't know if there's anybody else who actually does anything like what he does. The fourth grade in New Jersey, even since I was in school, is really the only year where you do a concentration of New Jersey studies, and he really brings it to life. He fills up half the playground area with his crafts. The kids realize that it is real—that this man is a real Native American."

**Learning is Fun!**

From the fourth grade on up, I make sure the kids have fun. If they are setting a trap, I ask for three Lenape trappers. I refer to them as Lenape because I am trying to get them to visualize themselves as Lenape Indians. I have them beating the drums, shaking the rattles, and I dress them up as coyotes and deer. I show them how to stalk the deer by disguising themselves as coyotes. I show them how to set the various traps, and I tell them they are Lenape trappers setting these traps. Then, I'll put the raccoon skin on one, and that person will be the raccoon that sets off the deadfall trap. It's fun, and I get them to use their imaginations.

I'll say, "I would like you to try and visualize in your mind's eye that when you came to school this morning there were no roads, no school buses, no vehicles, no stores, no houses, or hospitals. Everything you need to survive: water, food, clothing, shelter, and medicine, you had to get from the forests, fields, creeks, swamps, and rivers. That was the world the

Lenape people lived in." The Lenape didn't have stores. I explain that they had to turn to the forests and Nature to get what they needed. That's why the Lenape people protected those resources.

I'll say, "They tried to never overharvest, to never take more than they needed. They always put something back in its place to maintain a balance between what was taken and what was given back."

As an example, I tell them the story of how my grandmother taught me. When I was four years old, she took me into the forest to gather nuts, berries, acorns, and mushrooms. Sometimes she dug into a chipmunk's nest to take some of the nuts it had stored for winter food, but she always put corn in its place. I use that as a visual example to show how we maintained that balance. She made sure that chipmunk had enough food to carry it through the winter months.

*She was teaching me that as we take from the Natural World, we also put back.*

At other times, I will explain the Harvest Ceremony. When we harvest something, be it animal or plant, the sprinkling of tobacco is used as a thanksgiving. I noticed that these teachers focus in on that, I guess because it is so different. They told me that it often comes up afterwards when they have their discussions. I always try to make them understand it is important to honor the Earth.

### Life in the Bay: Children's Beach House

Children's Beach House in Lewes, Delaware, draws students from all over Delaware and Maryland. They learn about the ecology of the bay and ocean and do Nature-based projects. It's a year-round school, but they don't have permanent students; their students come from other schools. I am treated like somebody special down there. It is one of the first schools in Delaware that had me do a program. It was an old motel when I first started going there, and about five years ago they got some grant money: five million dollars. They constructed a new state-of-the-art building. It has elevators, which I am grateful for because I always had to drag all my crafts up the steps. The whole side facing the bay is glass. It's really something to see. It has live-in facilities for the students, a big dining room, and nurse's quarters. A lot of volunteers work there. They have their own beach where they take the students down to walk. They gather shells and the different marine animals to learn about the life in the bay. They are doing a tremendous job.

**Native Themes: Sanford School**

The Sanford School in Hockessin, Delaware, is exceptionally good. It is very large and laid out like a college campus. I think the grades go from preschool to high school. It's very upscale: the teachers and students are sharp. A while back, I went there to do a program and each class had a different native theme. They set aside areas and set up villages of different tribes. For the Inuit, they used the ends of plastic milk cartons as ice, and it looked real. I had to duck down and go through a low tunnel that opened to a room. The room simulated the interior of an igloo. As I stooped over to go through the entrance, I could feel the cold. They must have used fans or turned up the air conditioning. On the inside, they had harpoons, fishing spears, parkas, soapstone oil lamps, and bone utensils that are normally found inside an igloo. I could feel a chill in the air like I was in a real igloo.

I went to another class, and they had a room for the Western Plains Indians. It was set up like the interior of a tipi. There was a quiver hanging with arrows, a bow, and a lance. They had drums and different animal skins on the floor. I almost felt like I was in a real tipi. For the Eastern Woodland Indians, they set up the interior of a wigwam. The effort they put into trying to make it look authentic was tremendous! It showed their enthusiasm. It was a spectacular display.

I did a program at the Delaware School for the Deaf. There was a lady who was an instructor, and I was amazed because as I spoke the instructor signed for the students, and they comprehended everything.

### The Name-Giving Ceremony: Tattnall School

The Tattnall School is located near Wilmington, Delaware. They have a Name-Giving Ceremony, and I have been privileged to be a part of it. The sixth graders had me come into the gymnasium and open the program with a prayer. I explained the importance of the ceremony. Then, the announcer shouted, "From the mountains of Montana: the mighty Crow," and they beat the drums. The "Crow Indians" danced in and took their place at the (artificial) council fire. They were barefoot and wore items such as feather headbands and vests.

Then, "From the shores of the Delaware: the Lenape Nation," and that group danced in and took their place at the council fire. They were dressed in the same manner.

The announcer shouted, "This is the Season of the Clacking Stones," and about 25 "Indians" clacked their stones together while one of them walked clockwise around the circle. The sound of those stones echoed loudly in the gymnasium, creating an amazing sound. Then, one by one, the students walked clockwise around the circle displaying a shield with a symbol representing their new Indian name.

The announcer said, "From this day forth, (Tommy Jones) will be known as Jumping Antelope."

They had the drumming and the chanting, and the shields they made had symbols showing their new Indian names. It was powerful. It was as close to being at the old council fires out in the forest as it could be. It was emotional for me because it was the first time I'd ever been involved with non-Indian children who put that much of themselves into the

ceremony. They really did their homework because every major tribe in North America was represented. Every one of those tribes would have been very proud because the ceremony was done as close to the old way as they could do it. They really made the Name-Giving Ceremony come alive.

The teacher's name is Mary Beth Howard. In the beginning, she was a little concerned. Being non-Indian, she was afraid she might offend me if she didn't put this together the proper way. But every Indian I know would be very proud of the way those students had put it together. I know I came away feeling very strong. Mary Beth Howard told me she wants to continue this program every year. To learn about each tribe they represented, they got their information from books as well as the internet. The internet must have a *lot* of information.

The children there were thinking about what I was saying and they communicated that to their parents. At the Name-Giving Ceremony, I had to flee because the parents were saying, "This is all my daughter has been talking about. I had to come and see this Quiet Thunder."

That teacher is dynamite. They have the most impressive classes I've ever come in contact with. The children are well disciplined and very astute. They hang on every word I say. The following year, when I was setting up in the music room, some of the students came in and by their comments really made me feel as though I had done something special. They were especially impressed by how humane the deadfall trap was, the fishing snare, and the simplicity of the pump-action hand drill. Mary Beth Howard said those students will carry this education and these memories with them the rest of their lives.

She does an exercise with her students where they go on a walk in the woods and have to find items she has hidden. Seventy-seven out of 90 students found them all, which is outstanding. They didn't do as well with anything that was above eye level because they haven't developed what I call scatter vision yet. That's where you take in not just the obvious things, but also everything around you: up, down, on the sides, and what's on the ground too. But 77 out of 90 is exceptional, and at the same time it is helping to promote Indian culture. She is a teacher who has that ability to set those students in the right direction, and they grow with these instructions. Those Tattnall students are like sponges, soaking up every morsel. I see it come back to me, so I know it's working. Because these kids are grasping what I am saying, they help me come out with more than I otherwise would.

## Sadness and Guilt: Sacred Heart School

The Sacred Heart School over in Bryn Mawr, Pennsylvania, is a private school that was previously an old estate. After my first program there, I was packing up in the late afternoon and I felt the presence of somebody in the room. I turned around and saw a young girl standing there. I remember she was in one of the freshman classes. She just stood there looking so sad, and then she started crying.

I said, "What's the matter?"

Finally she said, "I know you must hate us."

"No, I don't hate you or anyone else," I said.

She said, "But what we did to your people."

"You had nothing to do with what happened in the past," I said. "Take that out of your thoughts."

I felt sorry for her. That's one occasion where someone felt pain and sorrow because of what happened to the Indians in America. To be honest, that was new to me because I had never experienced that from a non-Indian person. People will say things like: "It's a shame what they did to the Indians," and they will commence to tell me about these things. So to keep it from getting out of hand I'll say, "Just about any third-grade Indian kid going to school when I was coming along knew about it and moved on."

**Parent Participation: Elwood Kindle School**

I think it was in the early 1980s that we talked about money and education. Sure, money plays a big part in how good the education is because the more money, the better the teachers. But it's not just about money. The Elwood Kindle Elementary School is an old brick building, and its students were as sharp as any I have met. They were disciplined and asked pointed questions. The reason was *parent participation*. When the school has a PTA meeting, the parents are there. If there are any functions going on, the parents and grandparents are there, and the students know what is expected of them. This parent participation is the key to the whole thing. It was a school that I always loved to go to.

When I came back to do a program for the fifth grade, I showed them how to make a stone tool. The material that I use can be found almost anywhere. Now, after fifth grade, the students couldn't participate. So, in the afternoon when I was loading up my truck, the sixth graders came over and showed me what they had made during the year. It was amazing. The first ones didn't look all that good, but I could see how they were improving. Some of those stone tools were fantastic!

*Once they realized that the technology was not beyond their capability, the sky was the limit.*

The idea was, first of all, to let them realize they *can* make stone tools. Then, they have to go out to the Natural World to find the materials: rocks along the streams and wild grape vines. That's the whole idea—to get them going into the Natural World to relate to these natural materials. That was always the highlight for me: the afternoon when those kids came in to show me the crafts they had made.

**The Web of Life: St. Jones Reserve**

This organization is dedicated to protect and educate about the Delaware River watershed. They have a museum about the marsh ecology. There is a boardwalk on the marsh with stations that describe the plants and wildlife that tie into the web of life. They show tracks that you will see in the mud and what animals made them. The students from various schools are bussed in and given a tour of the boardwalk and museum. The students learn about how the plants, crabs, and animals that live in the meadow maintain its ecology. Periodically, they will give boat tours on the St. Jones River for the public and the schools. Sometimes I am requested by a school to be a part of their program at the reserve. I have been giving my presentations there and also at the Blackbird Creek Reserve since 2007.

## Stream Water Education: Catawba Jamboree

In 2003, I was invited to participate in a big spring event, which was held by Egg Harbor Township Middle School in South Jersey. It was an offshoot of a water-testing program that Greg Vizzi brought to the school. He had proposed a water education school program to the National Park Service, and he received a grant to produce it. He worked with Dave Crawford, the senior science teacher, to develop a day-long field trip for the students. The purpose was to help them learn about their streams, watersheds, and test the waters.

Dave started up the Jamboree at Charlie Young's property. One of the streams they tested was on Charlie's land, which was over 300 acres. Charlie made his land available to Dave to bring in the other schools in the district. I set up my display next to a pond in the field among many displays the students had set up. Various classes came through all day. It was a beautiful outdoor setting. I returned every spring until 2010 when they discontinued the jamboree. I think it was because of the expense to bus all the students and teachers to Charlie's. By that time the jamboree had gotten very big—well over a thousand teachers and students participated or passed through. It was a successful event that spread the water -testing program to the other schools in the township. Greg told me it is still going strong in a couple of schools that set up a water habitat in their schoolyards.

**Watershed Education: Brandywine Trek**

Bob Holliday runs the Brandywine Watershed Regeneration Project. Its purpose is to promote the health of the Brandywine River and watershed, which is located in southeastern Pennsylvania and northern Delaware. He knew the history of the area but was missing the beginning before the colonial period. That's where I fit in with the story of the Lenape Indians. Bob works with the Coatesville schools and the Stroud Water Center. They conduct an educational program called the Brandywine Trek, presented each year in different locations.

My first program for Coatesville High School was at a beach on the Brandywine River. I was surprised the students showed such a high level of interest; they asked many pointed questions. Bob was impressed with these African American students. I think the similarities between the Native American and African American cultures drew their attention, like the loss of our native languages. The Wyeth family must feel it's a worthwhile program because they offered to host the event at the Wyeth estate on the Brandywine River. Bob sometimes organizes a canoe trip for the students down the Brandywine to the Wyeth estate. He has me present my program to the students every year. I really enjoy it.

**Learning About the Birds**

There is a project I brought into the school systems that is starting to catch on. I would like to see it get into a lot more schools. Bayside Prison in South Jersey has a program for the prisoners to make birdhouses. All you have to do as a school administrator or teacher is contact the prison and request 15 bluebird houses, or 12 bat houses, or whatever kind you want. The lumber is recycled, which alleviates pressure on landfills. The local businesses have contributed the machinery, and it gives the prisoners something constructive to do.

The schools that get those birdhouses have the students put them up in the schoolyard and around their homes. Some of the teachers are starting to work this into their curriculum where they ask their students, "How many birds can you identify by flight?" Or, "How many can you identify by sound?" Now that doesn't seem like much, but how many kids do you know in the third grade who can identify a bird by its sound? It gets a little competitive, too. Now they are becoming more acclimated to the birds, and they start to observe Nature more keenly, which helps them realize that there is a whole Living World out there. The overall scheme of this is to try to condition those young minds away from using a lot of poisons when you have an insect problem. Try to do it the natural way with birds.

*It's a small thing, but if you can show them that birds were the main way of maintaining that natural balance, you can get that young mind away from using poisons to kill insects all the time.*

Then they start to relate a little bit more to the Natural World. It's those young minds that we must encourage because older people are just too far gone. One of the questions I get asked is, "Do you prefer teaching older or younger people?" It's both, but fourth, fifth, and sixth graders are my main targets because they are right at that pivotal point where they are the most curious and excited about learning.

It's their world we are getting ready to leave them, and it's not a very good one environmentally. So, if I can get just one mind to bend a little, I'll feel really good. One teacher said she was aware of many students I had done programs for over the years who went into college and took environmental courses. She told me she believes that a lot of them took those courses because of what I taught them in the sixth grade. That really makes me feel good. Some of those students may be moving in the direction of protecting the environment.

### Waste Not

I use animal skulls in my displays, and I am trying to gather as many as I can. I've got deer, muskrat, squirrel, rabbit, and beaver skulls. A lot of my handcrafts are damaged from being exposed to the outdoor elements and packing and unpacking at various locations. I am hoping that in the future I will be able to get the State of Delaware to set aside a facility where I can set up my display rather than move it around. If that comes about, I can put those skulls on display and identify them with plaques. When the schools send their children, I'll take the plaques down and ask them if they can identify the animals.

A while back, a disastrous event occurred. Someone up at the canal had killed two deer: both were bucks. One was a spike buck with an antler broken off and the other one was a six-pointer. They had only taken the hindquarters and just left the rest to rot. I cut the heads off and buried them in my garden so that the soil would do its job of decomposition. I have also been burying rabbit skulls to use in my displays.

Well, somebody in the neighborhood has a black Labrador retriever that runs through my yard periodically, and he dug up one deer head. Fortunately, he only took the spike buck. The six-pointer was too big for him to carry, I guess, but now I have to find a different method. In the past, I have always used the soil for the deterioration of the flesh. Now I have to find some other way because this dog keeps coming around. Apparently, he has an excellent nose to be able to smell it because it was down under the soil in the garden. That soil is covered over with a lot of mulch and leaves.

## Oral History and Storytelling

Oral history is very important for keeping our traditions alive.

Because my people did not have a written language, our traditions and history were passed on by word of mouth. In most cases, an elder taught this knowledge to a younger person in the family. Because these oral histories were given in a relaxed, storytelling way, our young people were eager to hear them. This was an integral part of their social upbringing, especially at that learning stage. Living in the Natural World opened many mysteries and sparked their curiosity. Everyone heard their family and tribal histories. In some tribes, certain individuals were trained to memorize those histories so the information was given in a precise way. Much of this history was taught to younger braves, and in some cases younger women. Most of this took place during the Season of the Clacking Stones in the winter when the people spent more time inside their wigwams. It was an important time for teaching our tribal laws and history. It was our form of education, and a method of keeping this knowledge alive, which otherwise would have disappeared. Those teachers stopped periodically to have the student repeat what was said, making sure they were getting the same message. Much of this was word for word. Each spring, they reviewed everything to make sure the young people understood what they learned was correct.

During those turmoil times when the Lenape people were forced into different areas of North America, much of this tribal knowledge was either lost or not passed on. Many people were forced to move several times into other tribal areas. Eventually, the knowledge

of those larger tribes tended to displace that of the immigrant Indians. That's one way much knowledge was lost. Today, a lot has been recovered, but not all in its original form. Fortunately, some of these teachings are verbatim the way they had originally been spoken, such as our creation mythology and the laws dealing with lying and stealing. A lot of the information in our oral history contradicts what has been written in books. The Europeans who wrote those books often gave a tribe a different name than what they called themselves. For instance, many history books call the Lenni-Lenape "Delaware Indians."

Before European contact, in the old way, much of the knowledge was in story form. But in my childhood and lifetime, it was more direct. Storytelling had been lost over time and, as far as I know, has disappeared from my tribe in New Jersey. There may be some that still do it today, but the influence of the dominant society has undercut the story form. Generally, storytelling isn't as powerful today as speaking directly. People have less patience and are being drawn into the technology of flashy electronic screens and fast action figures.

During those times of turmoil when Andrew Jackson forced the eastern Indians westward, the people were not passing on information through storytelling because those were not relaxed times. The connection to their homelands and what they were familiar with was broken off. Instead of talking about life along a creek in a story, they spoke more directly about the tides, the different seasons, and what took place in a location they would be hunting, trapping, or passing through.

The only story I can relate to that is still done the old way is our mythology of the creation of this land, Turtle Island, and the creation of the Lenape people. I tell it the way it was conveyed to me. This story is powerful because it deals with the most sacred and important ingredient in a Lenape Indian's life: the *creation of the land*. The turtle represents Turtle Island, or North America. It also represents the beginning of the Lenape people. They were born from the roots of the first red cedar tree, which grew from that turtle's back. That is a message so powerful it stays with us, and it stays with me.

## The Whole Cycle

I am dealing with young minds thirsting for education about Indian ways and Indian understandings. The overall theme is the *sacred obligation* that was given to the Lenape people to protect Mother Earth. That's the message I leave with the students. It is an obligation I am passing on, maybe not as sacred, but as common sense.

*Just use common sense—we can't continue to do to the Earth what we are doing and expect it to sustain life.*

I want to get people visually interested in the crafts I make. The teacher at Children's Beach House called it brain candy. What they see is interesting to them. Then I try to present a program that is exciting, entertaining, enlightening, and leaves them with a responsibility to protect the Earth.

*I hope they come away with an understanding of who I am, where I am, and why I am.*

That's probably the whole cycle right there. If people realize my sincerity and think about what I say, I feel good. That young mind has heard what I've said and now is exploring and dealing with new ideas.

A teacher once told me, "If you can get a young mind to do that, then you are teaching." It's getting that mind to work. I didn't have enough education myself to understand that this is teaching. A lot of those teachers' remarks are helping me make that connection. If I had some kind of formal education, it would be a forgone conclusion. But today, these things are starting to connect, and it is fulfilling to me.

## I'm Off to College

I used to speak primarily in schools, but now I go to civic and religious organizations, churches, hospice, and pretty much any group that wants to hear me speak. I tailor my programs from preschool up to the university level. Around the late 1980s, I did a program on the Lenape Indians at the Dover Public Library for a teacher accreditation. Shortly after that, Baerbel Schumacher called me and identified herself as the Director of International Education at the University of Delaware. She had gotten my name from one of those teachers who attended my Dover Public Library presentation. She asked if I was interested in doing a program for Russians, Ukrainians, and Siberians.

I said, "Lady, I can hardly speak English!"

She laughed and said, "No, that's no problem. These people teach English in their homeland."

"Well," I said, "sure."

So the first time it was for the Russians, Ukrainians, and Siberians. Then the second year it was for those three, plus some Muslim nations that were a part of the Soviet Union. The third year, it was for even more of those Muslim nations; Afghanistan was one of them. But the fourth year I did it, they asked me if I would be interested in coming to the Ukraine to do my program. I was all for it if it wasn't going to be in the wintertime. My wife said I'd be crazy to go over there in the dead of winter.

In the meantime, they started to have all their problems with the embassies, especially with the Muslim nations. The Soviet Union had started to collapse. The U.S. State Department at that time recommended no unnecessary travel there, and I never heard any more about it. I enjoyed being with them; they were very fun-loving people. They brought something to my attention I wasn't aware of: a lot of those people in nations occupied by Russia were experiencing the same things that happened here to the American Indians.

*The government came in and tried to crush their culture, their religion, and forbade the kids to speak their own language.*

So I realized that we Indians weren't the only people that happened to.

## The Thrill of the Hunt

In my programs, many of the ideas I bring to the table are considered very controversial. They are meant to be because part of my function is to bring common fallacies to the forefront so people can examine them and say, "Well, I never knew that," or "I wasn't aware of that," or "I don't agree with that." To date, I've had very few people challenge me. The few times that I have been challenged, I felt very confident that those people went away with a better understanding—sometimes it was an entirely different understanding for them.

For example, every September there's a sportsmen's jamboree outside of Millville, New Jersey. It's located in the Pine Barrens. I have been doing this program there for over nine years. The first year they got me to do it, I was extolling the whitetail deer and how we used every part of the animal, not just the meat and the hide, but all the bones for tools, the toes for rattles, the sinew for sewing, and much more.

I spoke about how the hunt began the night before with fasting and the Sweat Lodge Ceremony. Then I talked about the hunter rising early in the morning, washing and rubbing aromatic leaves into his body to remove his scent. Then, how he prayed as the sun rose, asking for forgiveness because he must take a life. After taking that life, he gives an offering of tobacco.

I said, "We used every part of that animal to show the proper respect and let the Creator know that we take responsibility for that life." Then I showed everyone all the different things that were made from the animal's hides, bones, sinew, and all that came from the deer.

I said, "Taking a life is an awesome responsibility because the Creator created that life. Many hunters today kill just to put an antler trophy on the wall—they call this sport. That is commemorating killing as though it's honorable: there's no honor in taking a life." There were three young guys standing out in front of the audience, and they got a little upset with what I was saying; I could hear the grumbling. There were a lot of hunters in that area, and some of them let me know they weren't pleased with what I said. I can understand that.

Well, the idea of killing as a sport comes from kings and queens, dukes and earls, lords and barons. *They* killed for sport. The Lenape killed to live.

Later on that afternoon, as I was putting my crafts back in my truck, I saw two of those guys coming towards me. They were pretty good-sized men, much bigger than me, and a lot younger. I didn't know what to expect. I had a stone tomahawk lying on the tailgate I hadn't put away yet, and I made sure I was close to it. So they came up, and one of them said, "You know Dick, we got a little upset with what you were saying, and we took it personally. But after thinking about it, it made sense."

Well, because they are hunters, they thought about all the hides and bones that they and their friends threw away. When they saw the clothing, and the bone tools, and thought about what was involved, it sunk in and made sense to them. Perhaps they realized they were just hunting to show a pair of antlers. They've taken an animal from its environment, especially an animal with antlers, without any regard to the balance of the herd's population. I felt pretty good.

About three years later, around Christmas, I was doing a school program near the Hamilton Mall, which is on the way to Atlantic City. Afterward, my brother Jim Three Buck and I went down to the mall to go shopping. A guy came over wearing a beautiful buckskin jacket with a fringe. My eyes automatically focused on his jacket.

He said, "Dick, you don't remember me do you?"

I said, "You look familiar."

He said, "I'm one of those guys at the Sportsmen's Jamboree that got uptight with you."

I said, "Oh yeah, I remember." I could tell that buckskin jacket he wore was handmade, and boy it was a beauty. He was very proud of it.

He said his friends who hunt with black powder, shotgun, and bow now give him their hides and bones. They used to get thrown in the dump. He took us out to his truck and showed us a pair of mittens he made that came all the way up to the elbow with fringe and beadwork. He also cures his own hides. It made me feel good that somebody got the message.

### We Only Get This One Earth

My reason for speaking out is to make people aware that Indian people are still here and of our connection with Mother Earth. The cause I want to deal with is that we only get this one Earth, and we have not been kind to her. We've got little ones who have come into this world who did not ask to come into it. It is our responsibility to try to make it possible that they have a tomorrow, and that is based on trying to protect these resources *today*. Not tomorrow, but today—or we will not have a tomorrow's world. I love hearing about young people relating to and caring about the Natural World because this is the world we will leave to them.

When I go back to Mother Earth, I want to have a clear conscience that I met the *sacred obligation* given to my ancestors to protect the Earth. So, I want everyone to know that there were Indian people who lived here prior to European contact who took that seriously and protected this land.

*This is where my people lived, and died, and went back to Mother Earth to continue that natural cycle. We come from Mother Earth, and we return to Mother Earth.*

# 8.
# CONCLUSION: WHAT LIES AHEAD?

*"Only after the last tree has been cut down, only after the last river has been poisoned, only after the last fish has been caught, only then will you find that money cannot be eaten." -Cree Prophecy*

## The World As It Was

Prior to European contact, the Natural World here on Turtle Island was in balance. Because of that, there was *abundant life*. My ancestors, the Lenape people, had come to depend on that abundance and played an important part in maintaining it. The hardwoods produced acorns and nuts. The land produced all the variety of foods we needed and many kinds of fruits and berries, which we harvested for food and medicines.

The streams and rivers were brimming with fish. I've been told that at times they were so plentiful it seemed like you could walk across the creeks on their backs. In parts of the West, there were so many buffalo, they covered the land as far as the eye could see. This abundance was maintained because the people had a deep reverence for Nature—the Great Provider.

My people lived in accordance with the seasons. Living from season to season was a very healthy way of life. The Lenape were a very healthy and happy people.

*Living according to the instructions the Creator had given to us kept everything harmonious and in balance. That balance has now changed. Balance is what it was all about and is still what it is all about.*

Pure water is a life-giving force of health for maintaining and cleansing the body. The Lenape lands had a great abundance of pure, flowing waters, and the people could drink from almost any creek, stream, or river.

*Without water, there is no life.*

My people usually made their camps and villages on high ground overlooking moving water. They began their day at the stream and washed themselves with water and sand. As the sun rose, they turned to the East and said a prayer. Water was considered sacred because it flowed from Mother Earth and sustained the lives of the people and all living things. Today, pure water is getting scarce worldwide. Many rivers and lakes are going dry. Some rivers no longer reach the sea.

When I first started to hunt, I had a good friend, an elder named Woody Conquest. His property was in the country beside a hardwood swamp. He got his water from a spring on the edge of his property. On occasion, when I was hunting in that area, I stopped there and got a nice cool drink. He was usually out in the back working in his garden, and he always spent time with me. This man was well into his eighties. He still had every tooth, no decay, and he attributed that to the spring water. I've heard people say things like, "The water from a natural spring has medicine and power." As I got older I learned that medicine and power refers to the healing and health benefits of pure spring water. That natural water had no chemicals, no chlorine, and it's meant to be that way. *Water is life.*

## The Powers of Balance, Destruction, and the Brotherhood of Man

*Today, we have the power to destroy and the technology of destruction.*

For instance, we have machines that can drain swamps, whereas before industrialization, the swamps were left alone. Now we can easily destroy swamps and wetlands. So people began to destroy the wetlands, and that had a huge impact on migratory birds, the fish, amphibians, and all living things that depended on the wetlands. It caused an immense disruption to the Living World.

*It showed that when men developed the power to destroy the wetlands, they did it without thinking about the ecological damage it would cause.* The Lenape people sought to do as little disturbance to the Natural World as possible because they were connected to the land. They knew that if they altered Nature too much, it could bring on terrible repercussions.

*The balance of Nature is delicate; it's as soft as the spring song of a cardinal. That song creates vibrations that bring on the spring. It's as delicate and light as the footsteps of a bird upon Mother Earth.*

We understood that each time we interfered with Nature's balance we were tampering with the Creation, so we did that cautiously. Everything is designed with balance: the moon, the sun, the directions they travel, the seasons, the migrations of the fish, birds, and insects, those that sleep in the winter and awaken in the spring.

*The Creator gave us the power of balance—the understanding that we are a part of Nature and inseparable from it. By understanding that the Creation sustains us, we also realize our responsibility to maintain its balance. What befalls the Earth falls upon all of us.*

This natural system has been in place since ancient times. If there were any shifts in it, they were due to a master plan, not man. The moon does not have a choice; it does what it's been designed to do. Everything following the Original Instructions is doing just what it's supposed to do. We have balance within us—that's our power. But because we have free will, we also have the power to destroy. Consumerism, our system of consuming without thought, leads to overconsumption. That is why there's such a contrast between the *abundance* of the past, and the *scarcity* we have now.

*Following the Original Instructions will restore balance to our thoughts and our understanding of how to live in harmony with the Natural World.*

Whenever I speak before an adult audience, I first give an opening prayer. My prayer goes like this:

*Oh, Creator of All Life, we come here today as brothers and sisters.*
*We ask for a very special power, a very special prayer.*
*As we look down, the color is turning brown.*
*It is the Mother Earth, and her power is the floor.*
*As we look up, the color is blue. It is Grandfather Sky.*
*His power is the roof.*
*As we look to the North, the color is white.*
*Its power is wind, cold, snow: endurance.*
*As we look to the East, the color is red.*
*Its power is light, warmth, and the promise of a new day.*
*As we look to the South, the color is green.*
*Its power is the changing of the seasons, to help things grow.*
*As we look to the West, the color is black. Its power is the Spirit World.*
*In between, the colors are red, white, yellow, and black.*
*And our power is Balance.*
*Oh, Creator of All Life, help us with this power, for we are failing.*

This brings the understanding that we are all brothers and sisters and are in this together, like it or not. That is why all cultures are important. When I hold my arrow up, I explain that the four color bands represent people on Mother Earth living side by side in peace *as brothers and sisters*. I believe the Creator has meant for us to be that way—in balance with each other. If we come to that realization, we can restore our balance and restore the Natural World. When I refer to an audience as brothers and sisters, I've come here to embrace them as brothers and sisters. Embracing people—male and female—breaks down any barriers. When I approach an audience that way, it takes out all the problems.

When we part, we don't say goodbye; we say, "làpich knewël," this means, "till we meet again." This implies that our connection is unbroken and a continuing part of the cycle of life. I present my point of view as a traditional Indian to expand people's understanding of Lenape culture. I am careful not to make a statement as a challenge. One person could become defensive and take me off track, then I will accomplish nothing. I think that extending the hand of brotherhood opens the door for others to do the same. If I back someone in a corner, he's not going to extend that hand of brotherhood, it's going to be a fist.

So as I travel and get older, I am trying to make life a little bit better, not just for me, but also for my children and grandchildren. It's often just little things. Sometimes it is just saying, "Hey, how are you doing?" It brightens my day, and I have come to realize that it brightens other people's day. I find that in most cases people will treat me the way I treat them. Any little thing I can do to help bring people closer together is an achievement, especially with all the conflicts here and throughout the world.

Before I go back to Mother Earth, I want to be able to look at my life and say that it was all worthwhile.

### We Are All In This Together

I try to convey ideas that people can deal with—simple things that everyone can do. Everyone can recycle; it saves dollars and cents, and it makes common sense. I would like people to look at this as a common sense obligation.

*Common sense says we can't continue to abuse the Earth as we've done in the past.* I believe that over the generations we have become conditioned away from common sense. It's not about going back to the Indian lifestyle of the past and living in a wigwam. That's not the world we live in. It's about using the natural energy sources: Grandmother Sun and Grandfather Wind. These sources of energy are natural and not destructive. The technology is here. Now it's getting people to use the technology, otherwise we continue to use fossil fuels.

Hopefully, our young educated minds will have the ability to take this knowledge and put it to good use. In order for this country to survive, we have to educate young people to use this technology to ensure we have a *sustainable* future. We must help them understand that they are included in this.

**Traditional Ways**

For Indians, there are still some problems today, and I believe there always will be, but life definitely is a lot better for most Indian people now. I'm sure we have some of the answers; no one has all of them.

*I've said before that I believe the traditional North American Indian is the living conscience of this nation.*

There are not many traditional Indian people around anymore. However, I do see some positive things happening, especially with some of the younger generation. Urie Ridgeway of the Nanticoke Lenni-Lenape Tribe of New Jersey was raised by his mother and father in the traditional way. He is bringing fresh leadership and cultural awareness to the tribe. Billy Redwing Tayac took him under his wing and introduced him to the Sundance when he was young. He has several children who he includes in his traditional activities. He established a dance and drum group called the Red Blanket Singers. They are growing in popularity in New Jersey and Delaware. He's an excellent speaker and officiates the dances at the powwows. He explains the purpose and meaning of each traditional dance. He speaks to different groups and talks about the tribe, what it is accomplishing, and where it's going.

There is a small group of traditional Lenape Indians in the Cheswold, Delaware, area and some young people who are showing interest in learning about our culture. Chief Dennis White Otter Coker heads the Lenape Tribe in the Cheswold area. He has reached out to the youth there. He leads a youth group and organizes a summer youth program every year. A while back, he asked me to be a part of their Name-Giving Ceremony. At that ceremony, I spoke to the entire group about importance of Mother Earth.

Sometime after that, Chief White Otter had a two-week summer program where they stayed at one of the state lodges near Bombay Hook. They went on Nature walks and had me come and do my program. That night, Chief White Otter showed the movie *Avatar* to the group. The next day he gave a talk about how it illustrates what is happening to our environment, who is behind it, and the role they play. That movie pretty much shows just what has happened here to the Indian people. So this is a strong program for educating our young people. I believe it will help our traditions to continue into the future.

*It has to pass on to the young people. They will be the ones who will need these traditions for the world they will live in.*

The Nanticoke Tribe in Millsboro headed by Chief Natosha Norwood Carmine is in the process of establishing their traditional ways. She has a vision for her people that I hope will materialize—that they will understand *who they are, where they are, and why they are*, as traditional Indians.

**The Gift**

I feel compelled to pass on this knowledge that I have. Both of my grandsons, Avery and Tyler, seem very interested in what I do. They sometimes assist me when I do my cultural programs. Avery even gives the opening prayer for me on some occasions. So I feel fortunate that I have grandsons who might very well carry my knowledge and programs into the future.

I know there's going to come the day when I'll have to face west, and the flag, which is black. I know not when, but I know this day is coming. When this day arrives and the

Creator looks down upon me and says, “Quiet Thunder, what did you do when you walked upon Mother Earth?” I want to be able to look with straight eyes and open heart and say, “I have tried to stand by that *sacred obligation* you gave my people to protect Mother Earth.” *Each footstep upon this Earth is a silent prayer. A Ho Ka!*

## Additional Thoughts by Marcia Adams and Greg Vizzi

The life of a Native American Indian conjures up many distorted mental pictures for most people. The Indians of today are working to dispel the stereotypes placed upon them. Prior to European contact, they had no concept of money or ownership. They shared everything they had with the first Europeans who came to this land. Everything they needed for survival was provided by Nature.

While the government has granted them token recognition as a minority, it is the Indians themselves who have opened their own universities, become congress members, and have worked tirelessly to see the fruition of the National Museum of the American Indian in Washington, DC. The successes by these special people have been accomplished on their own initiative.

The American Indians today have a fierce pride in their country. They have fought in every war this country was engaged in and died beside soldiers whose grandparents' generation had forced them from their land. In fact, the Indians' reverence for the land is so sacred that whatever they took from the land was always replaced. They were the original recyclers.

So who is Chief Quiet Thunder and what is it like to be a Native American in the 21st century? As you read this book, you will get an education that cannot be found in any history book because this story comes directly from a genuine Native American. Chief Quiet Thunder has kept the original beliefs of his people, and he has not sacrificed his heritage to peer pressure. The message of his people comes at you straight from his heart.

In his own words, he prefers not to dwell on the murky past, but rather to explain and perhaps dispel centuries of misconceptions about their customs, culture, and religion. Because of the vast knowledge he has of his own people and the powerful presentation he makes, Chief Quiet Thunder is in high demand as a speaker and educator. Soft-spoken and unassuming, he brings to his program hundreds of handmade artifacts, which he hauls in and out of his pickup truck. Children and adults linger after his program offering to help him load up his truck to spend a few more minutes with this very special person.

Highly acclaimed by the Delaware Teachers Association and the New Jersey Education Association, his program has been adopted as part of their school curriculum. His list of accomplishments, awards, and appearances are far too many to include here. But as an example, when he spoke before the United Nations on International Cultures, he received a standing ovation. He has taught first graders in elementary schools and graduate students at universities. Hundreds of school children have written him letters of thanks for coming to their schools, promising to remember what he taught them for the rest of their lives.

He was on the welcoming committee for the King and Queen of Sweden on their visit to the East Coast. The United States Information Agency invited him to speak to a group of foreign educators at the University of Delaware. After the program, the chairperson solicited comments on his presentation from the audience. A sampling of those comments follows: "One of the most impressive and touching meetings, the class was great, exotic and unforgettable, it was one of the most exciting meetings of my life, and I was greatly impressed by his wisdom."

The chief admits that at some gatherings there will be a skeptic or two, but his tactfulness and delightful sense of humor can diffuse any challenge. Even outdoor sportsmen who fiercely defend their right to "enjoy the thrill of the hunt" have done some rethinking after hearing the chief speak. His ability to laugh at life and at himself is indeed a rare quality. When asked if he had ever killed a cowboy his reply was, "John Wayne gave us a lot of trouble."

This very humble man has a keen insight into highly controversial topics. His enthusiasm for his subject captivates his audience, and if enthusiasm is contagious then those who hear him are truly infected by his message. Should you ask people if they know Chief Quiet Thunder, their first response would most likely be an almost whispered and reverent question, "Have you heard him speak?" So, here now is your chance to "hear him speak" his story.

-Marcia Adams

Like many kids growing up in the 1950's and '60s, I would rather have spent my time outdoors than sit in a classroom. I wandered the backwoods, fields, and streams of southern New Jersey. I canoed and camped in the Pine Barrens, the largest wilderness on the East Coast. In my explorations, I uncovered a mystery: arrowheads, spearheads, and other primitive tools, as well as broken pottery—evidence of an ancient people. I wondered who they were and how they lived.

History class never mentioned the native society that once existed here. As I grew up, I learned through other sources about the Indian people who occupied New Jersey. Often incorrectly referred to as the Delaware Indians, they called themselves the Lenni-Lenape. They occupied a vast territory consisting of the entire state of New Jersey, extending into northern Delaware, eastern Pennsylvania, southern New York, and western Connecticut. They also occupied a part of northern Virginia.

I wondered what happened to them. Then, much later, I wondered about another mystery. How did the Lenni-Lenape people manage to live sustainably in their homelands for thousands of years without depleting their resources?

One day I attended a Columbus Day Festival at the Rankokus Indian Reservation near Mt. Holly, New Jersey. Dick Quiet Thunder Gilbert, a Lenape Indian, was giving a presentation. He had reconstructed a village setting along a wooded area. He had animal pelts stretched on wood frames, dozens of beautiful bone and stone tools, painted drums, clan shields, and other handcrafted items on display. Behind him was a dugout canoe he and his brother had carved from the trunk of a giant tulip poplar tree.

He walked slowly and gestured expressively, while speaking in a soft, relaxed tone. As I listened to his stories, those childhood mysteries began to unravel. When I was growing up, my heroes were the American Indians—master woodsmen who lived as free men in the wilderness. We all assumed the Lenape Indians were long gone, yet before me was a living Lenape Indian who grew up in New Jersey!

That first meeting took place over 30 years ago. We kept in touch over the years and became good friends. I was honored to continue and expand the work of Chief Quiet Thunder's autobiography begun by Marcia Adams, a historian from Delaware. The Lenape culture is unique and different in many ways from the western Indian tribes. The Lenape were peace-loving people who once thrived in our now densely populated state, but little has been written about them from their own point of view.

This book does not speculate about their life from an archaeological or academic worldview 500 years after the fact. It is based on the ancient practice of oral history: a tradition of passing down historical knowledge through family, friends, and elders. It is knowledge of their culture: family and social relations, education, tribal laws, religion, spiritual practices, and their relationship to the Earth. The primary story is revealed through Chief Quiet Thunder's own family lineage and oral history. He does not intend to paint the same picture for all the Lenape tribes, as each tribe had its own customs, ceremonies, and circumstances.

As Chief Quiet Thunder explains, "One size does not fit all. They were not restricted in that way—there was this diversity."

Tribes were independent and had the freedom to adapt to changing conditions and social requirements. However, there are many universal themes common to all the Lenape and Algonquin tribes, and we have tried to present them. Chief Quiet Thunder has generously shared his culture and personal story, giving us a unique look into the indigenous past of his ancestors in North America.

More recently, other questions that bear investigation came to me: How could our colonial (and later, modern) societies allow so much destruction to our living environment in the short span of five hundred years? And how can we protect our Earth from further destruction? To answer those questions, listen to your heart as you learn about the ancient culture and wisdom of the Lenape people.

*"Today, indigenous people are at the forefront of environmental struggles worldwide, and they carry crucial wisdom for working toward a livable future on this Earth."*
*-Chloe Wang, Bartram's Garden Director of River Programs*

If we listen to our indigenous brothers and sisters and adopt a caretaking philosophy towards the Earth and each other, we can create a sustainable and abundant future. I believe it is imperative that we make this a top priority.

Please visit www.natures-wisdom.com for further information. -Greg Vizzi

INDEX OF CHAPTER SECTIONS

**1. Growing Up**



**2. In the Beginning: An Introduction to the People**

**3. The Natural World**



**4. Culture and Traditions: Past and Present**

**5. Seasons and Ceremonies**



**6. A Spiritual Way of Life**

## PHOTOGRAPHS AND ILLUSTRATIONS

Cover and book design by Greg Vizzi. Photographs by Greg Vizzi unless otherwise noted.

Copyright page; Red-wing blackbird, Edwin B. Forsythe National Wildlife Refuge, Oceanville, NJ.
Dedication page; Stream, Mantua, NJ.
Opposite contents page; Crafts by Chief Quiet Thunder.
Opposite acknowledgments page; Wetlands, Pine Barrens, NJ.
Introduction; Chief Quiet Thunder teaching.
Opposite Ch1; Chief Quiet Thunder teaching.
1 Male ruby throated hummingbird; NJ Pine Barrens.
2 Gray catbird, gray squirrel; NJ Pine Barrens.
3 Baby cottontail rabbit; Sweetwater, NJ.
4 Strawberry plant; iStock.
7 Chief Quiet Thunder's personal shield.
9 Annie; courtesy of Shanna Rosan.
10 Harry and Herman with deer, Anna; courtesy of Shanna Rosan.
12/13 Pintail ducks; Edwin B. Forsythe National Wildlife Refuge, Oceanville, NJ.
14 Chief Quiet Thunder demonstrating the deadfall trap.
21 Hognose snake, Edwin B. Forsythe National Wildlife Refuge, Oceanville, NJ.
22/23 Great blue heron in fog; Wharton State Forest, NJ Pine Barrens.
24 Great blue heron; Sweetwater, NJ.
26 Chief Quiet Thunder holding staff.
28 Red cedar tree and turtle shell on a deer hide; symbol of the Lenape creation myth.
29 Chief Quiet Thunder teaching.
33 Atsion Lake; NJ Pine Barrens.
34 Harrier hawk; Edwin B. Forsythe National Wildlife Refuge, Oceanville, NJ.
36 Thunder and Turkey shields.
40 Great Seal of the United States; 1904 die drawing; courtesy of Wikimedia Commons.
44, 45, 46 Chief Quiet Thunder teaching.
48 Wigwam frame; NJ Pine Barrens.
49 Curled leaf; NJ Pine Barrens.
50 Lenape Chief and William Penn; McCabe, James D.; The Pictorial History of the United States. Philadelphia: The National Publishing Company, 1877; courtesy of U.S. History online.
52 Chief Quiet Thunder and staff; Charlie Young's farm, Mays Landing, NJ.
55 Great egret; Edwin B. Forsythe National Wildlife Refuge, Oceanville, NJ.
57 Lenape homelands map; Courtesy of RuthAnn Purchase; Mitsumightous, Fiverr.
59 South Jersey Indian Trails Map; Courtesy of Chief Quiet Thunder; Mitsumightous, Fiverr.
63 Raising the U.S. flag on Mt. Suribachi on Iwo Jima during WWII; Joe Rosenthal, courtesy of Wikimedia Commons.
66 Maurice River; NJ Pine Barrens.
67 Chief Quiet Thunder teaching.
68 Spring peeper; field class with Dave Crawford, Mays Landing, NJ.
70 Red-wing blackbird; NJ Pine Barrens.
73 Chief Quiet Thunder storytelling.
74 Snow geese; Edwin B. Forsythe National Wildlife Refuge, Oceanville, NJ.
75 White lily; Lake Lenape, Atlantic County Park at Mays Landing, NJ.
76 Jim, Ralph, Harry, and Sport; courtesy of Shanna Rosan.

82/83 Sunset; Edwin B. Forsythe National Wildlife Refuge, Oceanville, NJ.
84 Makepeace Lake, NJ Pine Barrens.
85 Red fox; Brigantine, NJ.
86 Monarch butterfly; Wetlands Institute, Stone Harbor, NJ.
89 Whitetail deer doe; Assateague Island, MD.
91 Whitetail deer tracks, Chief Quiet Thunder tracking.
92 Whitetail deer buck; iStock.
94 Mockingbird; Mantua, NJ.
95 Blue jay; NJ Pine Barrens.
97 Canada geese family; Mullica River, Sweetwater, NJ.
98/99 Little egrets and glossy ibis; Edwin B. Forsythe National Wildlife Refuge, Oceanville, NJ.
100 Snow geese in flight; Edwin B. Forsythe National Wildlife Refuge, Oceanville, NJ.
102 Chipmunk feeding; Egg Harbor Township, NJ.
104/105 Tidal marsh; Edwin B. Forsythe National Wildlife Refuge, Oceanville, NJ.
107 Great Egret; Edwin B. Forsythe National Wildlife Refuge, Oceanville, NJ.
108 White throated sparrow on snow; Lake Lenape, Mays Landing, NJ.
109 Winter cabin; Galloway, NJ.
112 Cactus flower; Sweetwater, NJ.
114/115 Fence lizard; Wharton State Forest, NJ Pine Barrens.
117 Crows; NJ Pine Barrens.
119 Sunrise; Assateague Island, MD.
120 Crafts on deerskin by Chief Quiet Thunder.
123 Baby red-bellied turtle; Atlantic County Park at Lake Lenape, Mays Landing, NJ.
125 Chief Quiet Thunder and student's parent clacking stones.
126 Crafts by Chief Quiet Thunder on display.
128/129 Oyster catcher mother and baby; Edwin B. Forsythe National Wildlife Refuge, Oceanville, NJ.
130 Chief Quiet Thunder demonstrating the atl atl to a class.
132 Tulip poplar tree flower; Galloway, NJ.
133 Illustration of Lenape Indians launching a dugout canoe by Theodore Cornu, called "Departing from Camp." Courtesy of Marc Cheshire, Village Historian, Croton-on-Hudson.
134 Forest meadow; Trail near Batsto Village, Wharton State Forest, NJ Pine Barrens.
135 Chief Quiet Thunder showing a hoe made from a deer's scapula (shoulder blade).
136 The Three Sisters illustration by Digihandart; Fiverr.
140 Chief Quiet Thunder holding a bow.
143 Chief Quiet Thunder holding an arrow, showing personal colors.
146 Three quarter Moon.
147 Chief Quiet Thunder demonstrating how to use the ancient pump-action drill for making wampum beads.
148 Wampum belt of the Penn Treaty (Treaty of Shackamaxon); Courtesy of The Encyclopedia of Greater Philadelphia (Online).
150 Brass hatchet/pipe.
151 Stream with falls; Appalachian Trail,

eastern PA.

152/153 Mallard duck family; Lake Lenape, Atlantic Co. Park at Mays Landing, NJ.

154 Painting (print); courtesy of Chief Quiet Thunder.

156 Stone axe on deer hide.

158 Cardinal and snow; Atlantic County Park at Estelle Manor, NJ.

161 Chief Quiet Thunder Drumming.

164/165 Batsto Lake in the spring; Wharton State Forest, NJ Pine Barrens.

168/169 Great blue heron; Lake Lenape, Atlantic County Park at Mays Landing, NJ.

170 Atlantic Ocean; Brigantine, NJ.

171 Whitetail deer on Charlie Young's farm; Mays Landing, NJ.

173 Fall leaves; Weymouth park, NJ.

174 Chief Quiet Thunder teaching a class.

175 Deer rattle made from a gourd.

176 Mask of Mesingwe made from a gourd.

178/179 Winter landscape; Atlantic County Park at Estelle Manor, NJ.

180 Handcrafted stone axes.

181 Winter landscape; Atlantic County Park at Lake Lenape, Mays Landing, NJ.

183 Young participant as a Lenape Indian.

184 Chief Quiet Thunder holding a Turtle Clan shield.

186 Whitetail deer fawn; Assateague Island, MD.

188 Chief Quiet Thunder Raising a staff.

189 Winter sunset; Batsto Lake, Wharton State Forest, NJ Pine Barrens.

190 Earth from space; courtesy of NASA.

191 Sunrise; NJ Pine Barrens.

192 Sunrise in fog.

194/195 Canada geese in flight; Sweetwater, NJ.

196/197 Landscape; Batsto River, Wharton State Forest, NJ Pine Barrens.

199 Fireside prayer with Chief Quiet Thunder.

201 Central Fire; Tracker School primitive camp, NJ Pine Barrens.

203 Turtle drum and drumstick.

205 Sweat Lodge; Tracker School primitive camp NJ Pine Barrens.

206/207 Sky and clouds.

208/209 Eagle vision (composite image).

210 Eagle close-up; Cape May Zoo, NJ.

211 Ceremonial feather fan.

214/215 Medicine Pipe and pipe bag.

218/219 Forest in fog; Atlantic County Park at Estelle Manor, NJ.

220 Chief Quiet Thunder and Medicine Bag.

225 Chief Quiet Thunder storytelling.

226/227 North American bald eagle in flight along the Susquehanna River, MD.

228 Bald eagle in a tree on the Susquehanna River, MD.

230 Chief Quiet Thunder and class at a Catawba Jamboree event; Charlie Young's farm, Mays Landing, NJ.

231 Chief Quiet Thunder teaching at a girl scout camp.

233 Chief Quiet Thunder teaching a class at a preschool.

234 Batsto lake landscape; Wharton State Forest, NJ Pine Barrens.

235 Marsh landscape; Edwin B. Forsythe National Wildlife Refuge, Oceanville, NJ.

236 Ghost crab; beach, Margate, NJ.

237 Black skimmers; Edwin B. Forsythe National Wildlife Refuge, Oceanville, NJ.
238 Chief Quiet Thunder and student; Sanford School, Hockessin, DE.
240 Shields and bear drum.
242 Chief Quiet Thunder and parent at a preschool program.
243 Osprey and sunset; Edwin B. Forsythe National Wildlife Refuge, Oceanville, NJ.
244/245 Great egret catching fish; Edwin B. Forsythe National Wildlife Refuge, Oceanville, NJ.
246 Chief Quiet Thunder teaching at a Catawba Jamboree; Charlie Young's farm, Mays Landing, NJ
247 The Brandywine River south of Hagley Mills, DE; courtesy of Bob Holliday.
248 Purple martins; Atlantic County Park at Lake Lenape, Mays Landing, NJ.
251 Chief Quiet Thunder storytelling in a school program in southern NJ.
253 Children at a preschool program in southern NJ.
255 Great egret, Edwin B. Forsythe National Wildlife Refuge, Oceanville, NJ.
258 Adolescent red-tail hawk; Atlantic County Park at Lake Lenape, Mays Landing, NJ.
259 Chief Quiet Thunder program display with banner showing Planet Earth, a NASA photograph from space.
260 Injured North American Bald Eagle (composite image); Cape May Zoo, Cape May, NJ.
262 Baby mallard ducks taking a bath; Atlantic County Park at Lake Lenape, Mays Landing, NJ.
263 Great Egg Harbor River; Atlantic County Park, Mays Landing, NJ.
265 Cormorant; Galloway, NJ.
266/267 Winter sunset; Batsto Lake, Wharton State Forest, NJ Pine Barrens.
268 Chief Quiet Thunder giving a prayer; courtesy of Chief Quiet Thunder.
271 Wind and solar farm at the ACUA Solid Waste Facility; Atlantic City, NJ.
272 Chief Quiet Thunder teaching at a Catawba Jamboree program; Mays Landing, NJ.
274 Chief Quiet Thunder and grandson Avery Rosan at a Brandywine Trek event.
275 Chief Quiet Thunder giving a prayer at a girl scout camp program.
276 Spring dogwood blossoms; Atlantic County Park at Lake Lenape, Mays Landing, NJ.

Made in the USA
Las Vegas, NV
13 January 2025

16302864R00176